WISE CHILDREN

ANGELA CARTER

NOTES BY MICHAEL DUFFY

 Longman

 York Press

D0543717

The right of Michael Duffy to be identified as Author
of this Work has been asserted by him in accordance with
the Copyright, Designs and Patents Act 1988

YORK PRESS
322 Old Brompton Road, London SW5 9JH

PEARSON EDUCATION LIMITED
Edinburgh Gate, Harlow,
Essex CM20 2JE, United Kingdom
Associated companies, branches and representatives throughout the world

First published 2006

10 9 8 7 6 5 4 3 2 1

ISBN–10: 1–405–83563–X
ISBN–13: 978–1–405–83563–3

Typeset by Pantek Arts Ltd, Maidstone, Kent
Printed in China

CONTENTS

PART FOUR
CRITICAL HISTORY

PART FIVE
BACKGROUND

PART ONE

INTRODUCTION

HOW TO STUDY A NOVEL

Studying a novel on your own requires self-discipline and a carefully thought-out work plan in order to be effective.

- You will need to read the novel more than once. Start by reading it quickly for pleasure, then read it slowly and thoroughly.

- On your second reading make detailed notes on the plot, characters and themes of the novel. Further readings will generate new ideas and help you to memorise the details of the story.

- Some of the characters will develop as the plot unfolds. How do your responses towards them change during the course of the novel?

- Think about how the novel is narrated. From whose point of view are events described?

- A novel may or may not present events chronologically: the time scheme may be a key to its structure and organisation.

- What part do the settings play in the novel?

- Are words, images or incidents repeated so as to give the work a pattern? Do such patterns help you to understand the novel's themes?

- Identify what styles of language are used in the novel.

- What is the effect of the novel's ending? Is the action completed and closed, or left incomplete and open?

- Does the novel present a moral and just world?

- Cite exact sources for all quotations, whether from the text itself or from critical commentaries. Wherever possible find your own examples from the novel to back up your opinions.

- Always express your ideas in your own words.

These York Notes offer an introduction to *Wise Children* and cannot substitute for close reading of the text and the study of secondary sources.

CONTEXT
Because *Wise Children* does not deal with events in chronological order, it may be useful to draw up a simple plan or time line of the significant events.

 QUESTION
Reread the first page of *Wise Children*. Make a note at each point where a theme or issue is suggested in the text. What other features did you spot on this first page that appear in the novel?

READING *WISE CHILDREN*

What was to be Angela Carter's final novel turns out to be a wonderful carnival of magic and realism crammed into one single day, as Dora Chance awakes to the expectation of something about to happen. Between the drab routine of the house she shares with her twin sister Nora and the joyful, all singing and dancing return in the late hours, Dora constructs and **deconstructs** her own story, which is inextricably linked to the history of the theatrical Hazard family. The story reaches back to grandparents she never knew and looks forward to a new life as adoptive grandparents to a new set of twins.

What starts out as an intended autobiography turns into a family history, but *Wise Children* is more than that. It is a memoir, a dramatic monologue, a romance, a fairy tale, a comedy of errors, a tale of mistaken identities and disguises of Shakespearian proportions, pantomime, **farce**, carnival, a real world where magical elements seem almost normal, a journey through the theatrical world (legitimate and non-legitimate), a story with many **voices**, but ultimately, as Dora signs off at the end, a novel in its own right. It is this variety that gives both Dora and her novel their enchantment and fascination.

Flashbacks over a period of more than a century, and within these flashbacks flashes forward in time, create a kaleidoscopic portrayal of the family's entrances and exits. The material is apparently filed and indexed and waiting to be ordered into the family history, but Dora's direct address to the reader invites one into a story that is told with little concern for the unities of time, place or action. The truth of the story lies with the teller. Dora admits more than once that she may 'misremember' and her recollections are often qualified by self-questioning. On many occasions she asks herself (and us the readers) whether such an event really happened in the way that it emerges in the telling (such as the episode on Brighton Pier in Chapter 2).

It is not so much the fact but the memory that is important. This maxim applies to much of what Dora tells us. In one of her many direct addresses to the reader she actually invites us to believe or

> **? QUESTION**
> The non-chronological **narrative** moves back and forth in no particular order, as Dora recalls events as they come to mind. Why do you think Carter has Dora do this?

disbelieve. In the context of the story, truth does not signify. Reality is interspersed with the magical. Events as harshly real as the war can be put to one side, although memories of the blackout do bring to mind the oddity of a zebra running down the street, while the fighting provides Melchior with another role as he 'turned into a war hero' (Chapter 3, p. 161) and allows Peregrine another mysterious exit, this time 'being heroic' in the secret service (Chapter 4, p. 164). Even Grandma Chance's death is lightly dealt with at the time, though the poignancy does return in Dora's mind. At the end of the day Dora considers that Melchior had a somewhat 'two-dimensional' look at his party (Chapter 5, p. 230), rather as one might describe the portrayal of a character in a novel or play. Indeed, rather grotesquely, his head takes on the appearance of an oversized papier mâché carnival mask. As Nora wonders if they have not been making him up all along, together they come to the conclusion that he may be 'just a collection of our hopes and dreams and wishful thinking' (Chapter 5, p. 230). Dora murmurs 'very profound' but does not pursue the matter, leaving the reader to consider its profundity.

The Cole Porter lyric 'Brush up your Shakespeare' on the copyright page invites the reader to be aware of the playwright's presence throughout the story on and off the stage or screen. The events in *Wise Children* often mirror the plot of Shakespearian plays. The deaths of Ranulph and Estella and Cassius Booth are *Othello* come to life. The marriage between King Lear and Cordelia cannot happen in the play *King Lear*, but off stage it happens twice. Tiffany's entrance on television to Tristram's puzzlement and dismay mirrors Ophelia's appearance before Hamlet's mother and uncle, the world of game show a **parody** of Shakespeare. The confusions, disguises and mistaken identities of *A Midsummer Night's Dream*, distorted as they may be in *The Dream* film, are further distortedly mirrored in the romantic entanglements on and off set.

More than this, however, Angela Carter allows Dora to weave Shakespearian phrases into the fabric of the story. Melchior, for example, prepares to 'strut and fret his hour upon the stage' as the language of *Macbeth* enters the narrative (Chapter 2, p. 71). This happens throughout the story, and it is not just Shakespeare who can be found within Dora's narrative. Carter as a novelist is, like

CONTEXT

Intertextuality is a device used by most writers in other genres as well as novels. It is the deliberate blending into a text of ideas, references, often actual words, to suggest a connection or parallel between the two texts. Its purpose – serious, comic, parodic, contrasting, contradictory, and so forth – will depend on the context.

CHECK THE NET

Visit **www.centerfor bookculture.org** to find this interview with Angela Carter by Anna Katsavos. It is not specifically on *Wise Children*, but there are some interesting ideas from Carter about fiction.

CHECK THE BOOK

Gina Wisker says in her book *Angela Carter: A Beginner's Guide* (2003): 'The novel has an immediacy and a lively tone, produced by its first-person narrator, Dora ... with unconventional, alternative versions of events and values.'

Fevvers the high-wire flier in *Nights at the Circus*, a performer, and she did admit in an interview to enjoying playing with the reader.

You will find in the novel references to poetry, plays, songs, folk tales, fairy tales, rhymes, jokes, pantomime and film that reflect Dora's wide theatrical experiences and her education in English by her one-time lover Irish, but which also create a rich text for the reader. The story expands with rereading as one recognises more of these references, some of which appear almost like throwaway lines. Passing the Oval cricket ground, for example, Dora at seventy-five reflects that she and Nora are 'doomed to a century' (Chapter 5, p. 230). At times, too, Irish or her native wit seems to have given Dora the ability to create clever, witty, pithy aphorisms that remind us of Oscar Wilde or Dorothy Parker. They are wonderfully quotable in the broadest sense of the word, and are perceptive comments on events or attitudes. You will find that after a first reading your subsequent visits to the text will be richer because your linguistic and literary experience has increased through notes, discussion and a more sophisticated awareness of what Carter is doing in Dora's novel.

Wise Children has a cast of thousands, so many that there is an **ironic** dramatis personae as an endnote. It clarifies who is who in the story, but also, rather like the credits at the end of a film, includes virtually everyone. It is the novel's final parting parody. The confused real identities and secrets of the Hazard family have been explained, but then they are immediately questioned. The questions turn the reader back into the story. Are we to begin again? Certainly in studying the novel we must. Within the world of the novel, things do begin again, as the house of Hazard is reconstructed and regenerated when Nora and Dora adopt the new twins and become the new adoptive Grandma Chances in Bard Road.

In the story Carter explores several significant themes:

- patriarchalism

- legitimacy and non-legitimacy in its various forms

- illusion and reality

- decline of cultures and ways of life

Carter uses a first-person narrator but the novel is **polyphonic** (has many voices). Do not be fooled by Dora's drawing you as the reader into the story. One reference, explained in more detail in **Themes: Legitimacy and non-legitimacy,** has Peregrine calling Irish, his collaborator on the script of *The Dream, 'mon semblable, mon frère'* (Chapter 3, p. 118). The lines are actually from a Baudelaire poem, suggesting that the reader is a part of the writer's guise. First-person narrative always demands that the reader judges carefully what the narrator is saying. The language of *Wise Children* is a rich field. There is the formal, consciously literary style that Dora has been taught to use, but there is also the real speech of London. This means that literary **allusion** is woven into the story and colloquialisms, asides, slang and profanity colour the prose. Dora's tale is lively, engaging and blends serious art with a comic exuberance. Her philosophy of life is a blend of her own 'What a joy it is to dance and sing!' and Grandma Chance's 'Hope for the best, expect the worst', and these two maxims give the story its impetus and its appeal.

QUESTION
What do you find unconventional in Dora as a narrator?

PART TWO

THE TEXT

NOTE ON THE TEXT

Angela Carter's last novel, *Wise Children*, was published late in 1991 by Chatto & Windus Ltd, only a few months before she died of cancer. The edition used in these Notes is the paperback published by Vintage in 1992 and reprinted numerous times.

CONTEXT

Salman Rushdie, a friend and fellow user of **magic realism** in his own fiction, said that *Wise Children* was Angela Carter's finest novel. 'In it, we hear the full range of her off-the-page, real-life voice' ('Angela Carter, 1940–92: A Very Good Wizard, a Very Dear Friend', *New York Times Book Review*, 8 March 1992).

SYNOPSIS

The stories that Dora will tell – her own and the history of the Hazard family – are convoluted to start with. Given Dora's chatty style and her ability to go off at a tangent at the drop of a name, it is difficult to give a synopsis without going into the detail that makes up the summaries that follow. What may help the reader is a general indication of the substance of each of the five chapters that make up *Wise Children*.

Chapter 1 deals with Dora's intentions as a writer. It reveals the past history of the theatrical Hazard family as performers of Shakespeare at home and, significantly, on tour abroad, taking culture to the world; and it introduces us to an array of characters from both the Chance family and the Hazard dynasty, past and present. We meet Lady Atalanta Hazard (now known as Wheelchair), first wife of Melchior Hazard, Dora and Nora's father; and we are given a glimpse of Melchior's tangled marital affairs and introduced to his legitimate offspring: twins Saskia and Imogen by Lady Atalanta; and twins Tristram and Gareth by his third and current wife, My Lady Margarine. On the Chance side, we are introduced to Grandma Chance, Dora and Nora's guardian, who adopted them on the death of their mother in childbirth. Their adoptive family has extended over the years and now includes Tiffany, their goddaughter.

Dora and Nora's preparations to attend the one hundredth birthday party of Sir Melchior are interrupted by Tristram bringing news of Tiffany's disappearance. Her distressed state has been captured on a video of the game show hosted by Tristram, and as they watch the show and learn the story behind Tiffany's disappearance, so Dora reveals the history of their families in a series of flashbacks, digressions and asides.

Dora's paternal grandfather, the great actor Ranulph Hazard, had murdered his wife and lover before killing himself in a New York hotel. The three were playing in *Othello* and life imitates art – not for the last time – in this story. Twin boys Melchior and Peregrine, orphaned at ten, eventually make their own way in the world. Melchior runs away to become an actor and achieves fame and status. Peregrine simply runs away into the unknown and makes his fortune. Nora and Dora, illegitimate daughters of Melchior and a servant, Kitty, who dies in childbirth, are brought up by Grandma Chance. Peregrine, who comes and goes unannounced, fulfils the role of father in the family that Grandma Chance seems to have invented. There is a memorable day out in Brighton, complete with beach picnic and a pier show. Peregrine enables the girls to meet their real father, who is appearing at the local theatre, but he fails to acknowledge them. Back in the present time, they receive news that a woman's body, which they fear must be Tiffany's, has been found in the river.

Chapter 2 describes the childhood of the twins. The reader will now have realised the non-chronological nature of the **narrative**. Dora and Nora see their father from a distance in a theatre and he becomes a romantic figure for them. At an early age they become a part of the theatrical community, but in the non-legitimate world of pantomime and music hall. Melchior produces two more 'legitimate' daughters, twins Saskia and Imogen. On tour Nora is seduced by the pantomine goose, the first in a long line of romantic entanglements. Dora, less forward than her twin, falls in love with one of Nora's boyfriends, and eventually persuades Nora to exchange identities and lend him to her for a night of lovemaking. Nora and Dora are invited to be singers and dancers in Melchior's Shakespearian revue *What You Will*. The celebrations at Melchior's house turn into a riotous carnival as the house burns down. However, an American producer has decided to take the cast to Hollywood to make a film.

> **CONTEXT**
>
> In Shakespeare's play *Othello*, Othello is driven to believe that his young wife, Desdemona, has been unfaithful to him. In a jealous rage he kills her and then commits suicide.

> **CONTEXT**
>
> The worlds of illusion and reality are important features of theatre and real life in *Wise Children*, as is the whole question of true and false identity. Twins crop up frequently in the comedies of Shakespeare, as do the themes of disguise and mistaken identity; it is worth looking at Shakespeare plays such as *Twelfth Night*, *As You Like It*, *Two Gentlemen of Verona* and *The Comedy of Errors* in order to see all the parallels in Carter's novel.

CHECK THE FILM
A good film guide such as Halliwell's will give details of the real-life 1935 production of *A Midsummer Night's Dream*, together with comments about the adaptation and its critical reception.

In Chapter 3 the action takes place on and off the film set in Hollywood. Nora falls in love with Tony, an Italian, while Dora is educated by her older lover Irish, who schools her in writing and literature. *The Dream* turns out to be an extravagant, expensive 'kitsch' version of *A Midsummer Night's Dream*. Melchior's ambition is to take Shakespeare to America as his father had done. However, the producer, known as Genghis Khan, has the money and the power to do as he wishes. His tyrannical rule over his film kingdom, however, cannot prevent his second wife, Daisy Duck (real name Delia Delaney), from having an affair with Melchior, Oberon to her Titania. When news of Daisy's pregnancy is followed by her engagement to Melchior, and Lady Atalanta and Genghis are unceremoniously dumped, Genghis himself seeks revenge by proposing to Dora. These complicated romantic involvements off the set mirror the events of the play/film, and culminate in a triple marriage ceremony; but disguise (Dora switches places with Genghis's first wife, who remarries her former husband) and the intervention of Tony's mother ensure that the weddings do not go smoothly. Peregrine turns up on a white horse as Sheriff of Hazard, Texas, to perform the ceremonies. Grandma Chance appears to rescue them, and takes Nora and Dora home with her to Bard Road.

CHECK THE BOOK
Kate Webb in a footnote to her essay 'Seriously Funny: *Wise Children*' identifies some of the possible locations that would have been familiar to Angela Carter. They are possible inspirations for some of the fictional places in *Wise Children* (in *Flesh and the Mirror: Essays on the Art of Angela Carter*, edited by Lorna Sage, p. 339, note 20).

The return to England and the war are described in Chapter 4. After the war the differences between high and low culture are more prominent. Melchior becomes the great Shakespearian actor-producer. Dora and Nora pass through pantomime and the declining music hall into nude revues. They befriend Lady Atalanta. At a disastrous twenty-first birthday party for Saskia and Imogen, Peregrine reappears unexpectedly from South America, and Melchior announces his third marriage, to one of Saskia's friends. Peregrine returns to South America. Lady Atalanta Hazard, following a dispute with her daughters, falls and is confined to a wheelchair. Penniless, she is taken in by Dora and Nora. Back in the present time, the three of them prepare for Melchior's party.

Chapter 5 centres on Melchior's birthday party. They see Gorgeous George, a comedian they first saw in Brighton when they were little girls, and the man who played Bottom in *The Dream*; he is begging in the street outside Melchior's London home. Guests queue to greet Melchior. He finally acknowledges Dora and Nora as his daughters. Peregrine, missing for so long he has been presumed dead, appears suddenly, surrounded by butterflies. Tristram arrives but is still distraught. Peregrine theatrically produces a pregnant Tiffany from a trunk, but she rejects a grovelling Tristram. In the confusion that arises when it becomes clear that the birthday cake has been doctored by Saskia, Dora precipitates confessions all round when she reveals that Melchior is not the father of the twins Saskia and Imogen. Peregrine confesses that he is their father as Lady Atalanta reveals the truth about her infidelity. Saskia and Imogen reject Peregrine. In the confusion Dora escapes upstairs with Peregrine to make love. As a final trick he produces twins from his pocket, supposedly the children of Gareth, the Jesuit missionary. Nora and Dora return home with the twins, a boy and a girl, to Bard Road.

DETAILED SUMMARIES

CHAPTER 1

PAGES 1–11

- Dora introduces herself and her twin sister and reveals her intention of writing her autobiography.
- This will encompass the history of the Hazard and Chance families.
- Their invitation to Sir Melchior Hazard's one hundredth birthday arrives.
- The present household of Dora and Nora, who are now seventy-five, which includes Sir Melchior's first wife, is described.
- Tristram, son of Sir Melchior by his third marriage, arrives with news of the disappearance of Tiffany.

Dora Chance introduces herself and reveals her intention of writing her autobiography. Dora and her twin sister Nora have been raised by Grandma Chance, but are in reality the still unacknowledged illegitimate daughters of the great theatrical figure Sir Melchior

CHECK THE BOOK
According to Gina Wisker: '*Wise Children*, Carter's last novel, is in the fashion of Shakespearean comedies: sprawling, filled with characters and whimsy, action and humour, escapes and fantasies, celebratory' (*Angela Carter: A Beginner's Guide*, 2003). You might find it useful to make a note of these elements as you read the novel.

QUESTION
In the opening pages of the novel Dora's zest for life, her self-deprecating humour and her essential good nature and decency, strikingly apparent in her loyalty to Wheelchair, are evident. Such characteristics, which she shares with her illegitimate twin, Nora, are sorely lacking in the legitimate daughters of Melchior, Saskia and Imogen. What purpose does this negative comparison have?

 QUESTION
Why does Dora begin with a riddle, the sort you might find in a Christmas cracker? What is the idea within the riddle?

Hazard. They are two former singers and dancers, showgirls from the non-legitimate side of the theatrical world.

Today is the twins' seventy-fifth birthday, and Dora has a feeling that something is about to happen. Invitations to the celebration for Sir Melchior's hundredth birthday arrive. Wheelchair, the twins' basement lodger, whose identity is yet to be revealed as Lady Atalanta, the first wife of Sir Melchior, will attend with them. There is the suggestion that all the skeletons in the family closet may be revealed today. The complicated family tree of the Hazard family begins to be drawn.

The fact of the twins' identical appearance yet differing personalities is introduced. Dora recalls their theatrical career in music halls and, later, lower down the theatrical scale, the revue shows.

Their loyalty to Wheelchair is described in a strange blend of sentiment and apparent indifference. Wheelchair's twin daughters, Saskia and Imogen, some years younger than Dora and Nora, have disowned their natural mother, though their legitimacy within the Hazard family will be called into question later in the **narrative**.

The tedium and routine of everyday existence are broken by the sudden arrival of Tristram Hazard. Tristram is the son of Sir Melchior by his third marriage, and twin brother to Gareth, the Jesuit missionary. Dora asserts that she and Nora are, in fact, Tristram's half-sisters, though, in her words, 'from the wrong side of the blanket' (p. 8). Tristram is the host of a dreadful television game show. He is distraught that Tiffany, his girlfriend and hostess on the programme, has disappeared. However, Tristram has brought a video of his show, which will reveal the circumstances leading to Tiffany's disappearance. Tiffany is clearly in some way connected to the Chance family. As the video is about to be played and the circumstances revealed, Dora presses 'Freeze-frame' (p. 11).

COMMENTARY

A riddle, a conundrum about similarities and differences, appropriately and bluntly opens this novel, which is essentially about puzzles, surprises, parallels, double identities, juxtapositions, divisions, separations, comparisons and contrasts.

The narrator, with her distinct voice, establishes the narrative style with a strange blend of naive formality ('Let me introduce myself') and self-mocking realism ('Welcome to the wrong side of the tracks'). Dora's ability to deflate the serious to the comic ensures that the story is firmly rooted in the real world, which sits alongside the world of illusion that she and her family have inhabited for over a century. This world of the theatre encapsulates the late nineteenth and twentieth centuries and will range from legitimate theatre to the various illegitimate offsprings – pantomime, musical comedy, burlesque, song and dance, stage comedians, film and television.

Dora introduces her twin sister Nora, identical ('like as two peas') but not symmetrical: 'She said "Yes!" to life and I said "Maybe ..."' (p. 5). This pattern of twins, alike but disparate, is repeated throughout the history of the Hazard family with its proliferation of twins in different generations.

As Dora's story unfolds, several features of style emerge. In this section we have several examples of direct addresses to the reader, rhetorical questions, inconsequential interruptions, basic – even profane – language, trigger words which spring memory into action and take the story off in other times and places, an impressionistic cataloguing technique which characterises in swift images person, place or atmosphere. The listing or cataloguing frequently culminates in anticlimax or bathos. The world of the theatre becomes an integral part of the semantic field in the story. Dora, for example, is not merely born, but 'made my bow' (p. 2). References to theatres, plays and actual persons in the theatre and name-dropping provide a rich tapestry on which the Hazard family story unfolds.

The sympathetic background of a 'topsy-turvy day of wind and sunshine' (p. 3), on which the story begins (and ends, for the events do all take place within the one day), recalls the day of their birth, suggesting, as it does in Charles Dickens's *Great Expectations* (Chapter 17 recalling Chapter 1), that something is going to happen. A parallel coincidence is that this day is the shared birthday of Nora and Dora; Melchior, their father; Peregrine, his twin brother; and William Shakespeare himself.

CONTEXT

The various levels of 'legitimacy' of public performance – serious theatre, film (especially Hollywood), music hall, variety, pantomime, burlesque and nude shows – can be traced through the history of late nineteenth- and twentieth-century Britain and form an integral part of the story's backdrop.

CONTEXT

The casual references to real stars of theatre and film are numerous; on p. 2 alone Dora mentions Ivor Novello, Noël Coward, Fred Astaire and his sister Adèle, Jack Warner, Ginger Rogers, Anna Neagle, Jessie Matthews and Sonnie and Binnie Hale.

CONTEXT

Samuel Taylor Coleridge in looking at the ideas of fancy and imagination in *Biographia Literaria* (1817) coined the phrase 'the willing suspension of disbelief' to describe the reader's or audience's willing acceptance of the writer's imagination. You will find several references to this idea in Shakespeare's plays.

CONTEXT

Lochinvar was a romantic lover, the hero of a ballad included in a poem written by Sir Walter Scott (*Marmion*). The fair Ellen is about to be married to a villain, when valiant Lochinvar appears to rescue her.

The family names of Chance and Hazard (Dora's adoptive and natural families) play with this central idea in the story. Chance stretches the 'suspension of disbelief' and invites the reader into a 'real' world of theatrical coincidences. Dora's cry 'What a joy it is to dance and sing!' is a motto that rings out across her life. Her refusal to go 'gently into that good night' (p. 6) – the phrase is from a Dylan Thomas poem – is reinforced in the detail given to the clothes, the make-up and the enjoyment of a 'knees-up' and now their determination to attend the birthday celebration.

Dora's paradoxically sentimental nature is seen beneath the apparent air of indifference to their adopted Wheelchair, whom they have been 'storing … in the basement for well-nigh thirty years' (p. 7). Her real identity as Lady Atalanta Hazard, 'the most beautiful woman of her time', now contrasts with her reduced circumstances. She is reduced even to impersonal references – she becomes 'it' frequently; she is plugged into the television; she is 'greased' like a machine, though with bacon fat.

Tristram's arrival and his dramatic (maybe dramatised) distress is put into context by Dora's blunt reactions to his situation and his 'poxy' programme. Wheelchair rejoices in watching this awful show, but only in so much as she relishes the fall of the house of Hazard. Nora's **ironical** question 'What's biting young Lochinvar?' reinforces the general reaction (p. 9).

However, matters are taken more seriously when it is revealed that Tiffany is missing. The video recording of the show enables Dora to fill in Tristram's background. He is the grandson of Ranulph and Estella, son of Sir Melchior and, therefore, half-brother to Dora and Nora. Described as 'weak but charming', Tristram's role as presenter of a game show provokes Dora into commenting: 'Lo, how the mighty have fallen' (p. 10). The introduction of the video permits a neat break in the action, enabling Dora to clear up for the reader the complicated background.

GLOSSARY

1	*rive gauche, rive droite* left and right banks of the Seine
	diaspora migration of people to other communities
	And what does the robin ... thing? line from a nursery rhyme
2	**chorine** chorus girl
3	*Brief Encounter* film (1945) where the action takes place on a railway station
6	**Victory rolls** hairstyle popular in the 1940s; a victory roll was performed by a successful pilot
7	**Normal Hartnell** Norman Hartnell (1901–79), fashion designer; the name is deliberately parodied by Dora
10	**Busby Berkeley** American choreographer and director
	Ivory Novello Ivor Novello (1893–1951), actor, composer, songwriter and playwright

PAGES 11–21

- Dora provides more details of their family background.
- The story of her grandparents, Ranulph and Estella, is told.
- The deaths of Ranulph and Estella in a love triangle resembles the plot of *Othello*.

The story of Tristram and Tiffany is held on freeze-frame, as Dora provides more detail about her researches and her illegitimacy. She has no illusions about the circumstances of her birth – 'there was sod all romantic about *our* illegitimacy' – but does express a serious purpose, her desire to find an answer to the questions (hidden, appropriately, 'behind a curtain'): 'whence came we? Whither goeth we?' (p. 11).

A photograph of Estella, the twins' grandmother, takes the story of the Hazard family back to around 1870. Born into the theatre, Estella becomes a child actress. Dora's story leaps forward as she recalls her grandmother's stage career, with a brief reference to Estella's affair with another actor, Cassius Booth, then describes events surrounding her sudden death. Details of Estella's life on the stage are given, interrupted by various asides, for example the

? QUESTION
What is the effect of the pressing of the freeze-frame? What does it permit? Discuss the other techniques Angela Carter uses to control the non-chronological **narrative**.

 CHECK THE NET
London at this time had numerous theatres and music halls and there was a wide variety of performers. The decline of the music hall was yet to come. For some idea of the scale, visit **www.victorian london.org** and click on 'Entertainment'.

CONTEXT

Lewis Carroll
(1832–98) wrote
*Alice's Adventures
in Wonderland*
(1865) and
*Through the
Looking-Glass*
(1872). He was,
more significantly
in this context,
a pioneer of
photography,
taking portraits
particularly of
young girls.

gossipy reference to Lewis Carroll and the first mention of Irish, who, Dora tells us, will be important later in the story. The roles, the provincial theatres, the circuit of a life on the stage and on the move in the late nineteenth century contrast the glamour of the stage with the realities of life.

Estella eventually plays Cordelia, the faithful daughter of King Lear, played by the ageing Shakespearian actor Sir Ranulph Hazard. An amusing character sketch of Sir Ranulph follows. Thirty years older than his Cordelia and already thrice married, Sir Ranulph marries Estella.

A brief reminiscence of a visit to a record archive to hear Sir Ranulph's voice on a wax-cylinder recording allows Dora to muse on the past with its memories and the present with its realities of the basement in Bard Road and Tristram's game show on television.

Ranulph and Estella begin their American tour with a production of *Hamlet.* It is at this point that the twin boys, Melchior and Peregrine, are born. There are further asides to future relationships in the Hazard family (Melchior and Peregrine as 'fathers' to Dora and Nora, the first mention of the half-sisters Saskia and Imogen, and Tristram's brother, Gareth, a Jesuit missionary). We return to the marriage and the touring of Ranulph and Estella, retold by Dora via Peregrine's accounts from his mother. Dora briefly sums up Peregrine's restless, adventurous and somewhat mysterious life in a catalogue of roles and images.

Ranulph and Estella's touring continues with fame following in their wake – the naming of an ice cream sundae after Estella, a township renamed Hazard in New South Wales, a Hazard Street in Tasmania. The town of Gun Barrel in Texas is renamed Hazard in their honour (and is destined to figure later in the story). But Ranulph is losing his touch as well as his money. Estella stays with him and in Tucson makes him a cardboard crown, the original having been gambled away.

The final act in their marriage occurs in New York, where Cassius Booth is now a successful actor-manager on Broadway. Ranulph is offered the role of Othello; Estella will play his loyal wife,

CONTEXT

'Ice-cream Estella'
(p. 18) is a comic
allusion to peach
Melba, a dessert
named in honour
of the Australian
soprano Dame
Nellie Melba.

Desdemona; Cassius will play the villain Iago. Renewal of the affair between Estella and Cassius ends in their deaths at the hands of Ranulph, who in turn shoots himself – an echo of the *Othello* story.

COMMENTARY

Dora moves beyond autobiography to become the 'chronicler of all the Hazards' (p. 11). At the outset she reveals a serious purpose in her researches, searching through the 'archaeology' of her desk (p. 11). It is as if Dora is seeking the legitimacy of herself and her own story in this almost consciously sublime language. Lexical choice here is worth noting. The whole question of legitimacy/illegitimacy extends beyond family and theatre to encompass the legitimacy of the story. This multidimensional theme runs throughout the novel.

The issue of relationships between children and those giving them birth and raising them significantly omits the patriarchal figures, bypasses the mother and focuses on the grandmother. Their natural paternal grandmother is, as Dora says, 'the one fixed point in our entire genealogy' (p. 12), and it is the adoptive Grandma Chance, with no biological connection, who raises them. Love, 'genuine family romance', is set against duty and, still further back, against denial and betrayal. Carter adds to the works of feminist thinkers, notably Hélène Cixous (see **Feminism and post-feminism**), in challenging the **phallocentric** idea of origin and in her belief that another history can be told which destroys the stereotype of the father figure.

Dora's description of their paternal grandmother, Estella, is constructed from photographs, reviews, the obituary and the memories of others, notably Peregrine. With several asides (by now a familiar feature of the **narrative** style, alternately puzzling us with anticipated references to characters and situations we have not yet met or going back to explain or clarify), Dora presents a character sketch of Estella, the name as significant as that of her counterpart in *Great Expectations* – 'A star danced and she was born' (p. 12). The similarities to Judy Garland are pointed out by Kate Webb in her excellent essay 'Seriously Funny: *Wise Children*' in *Flesh and the Mirror: Essays on the Art of Angela Carter*, edited by Lorna Sage (1994). The life of an actress in Victorian England is described through the gradually ascending roles on stage, the

---

CONTEXT

It is likely that Carter chooses the word 'archaeology' deliberately here; she was familiar with Michel Foucault's work *The Archaeology of Knowledge*. In this and other works, Foucault, a twentieth-century French philosopher and historian, explores the nature of discourse. Part of his theory suggests that naming is the first stage in classification, which then leads to analysis, knowledge and finally power over the subject under investigation.

CHECK THE BOOK

Kenneth Anger's *Hollywood Babylon* (1975) is a useful guide to the lives of actual Hollywood stars and their references and allusions in *Wise Children*.

CONTEXT

In Shakespeare's play *King Lear*, Lear, king of Britain, divides his kingdom among his daughters. Two betray him, while the loyal Cordelia dies in attempting to save him. In the Hazard story, both Ranulph and his son Melchior play King Lear and marry their Cordelias.

glamour of stage and the squalor of life on the move from provincial theatre to theatre.

The significant moment in Estella's life comes when she plays Cordelia to Sir Ranulph Hazard's King Lear. The portrayal of Ranulph (who is destined to marry Cordelia – a situation mirrored in later events), is a blend of the great but unpredictable actor, unreliable at times on stage, even more unreliable in real life in terms of love and money.

Ranulph's mission is to spread the word, or rather the Shakespearian word, overseas, and there follows a description of their travels and performances in all corners of the British Empire and the New World. It is on their travels in America that the twins, Melchior and Peregrine, are born. Dora refers to them both as 'our fathers', the former the natural, the latter the one who acknowledges them as his own. The names of Peregrine and Melchior are more than coincidental to the tale, the former signifying a wanderer, the latter one of the wise kings in the Bible. The legitimate paternity of Melchior and Peregrine is more than doubtful, as Ranulph's three previous marriages and extramarital affairs had produced no issue, and Estella's liaison with Cassius Booth is euphemistically described in such a way as to leave little doubt.

The cardboard crown makes its appearance in the Ranulph–Estella story, just before its dramatic finale, as life once again almost imitates art – the deaths of Ranulph, the jealous; Cassius, the betrayer; and Estella, not the innocent in the affair. Dora's comment: 'But the play he picked on was, alas, *Othello*' (p. 20) warns us of what is to happen if we know the play. Othello, driven to jealousy by the treacherous Iago, kills Desdemona, his wife, stabs Iago and then kills himself. Here, Shakespearian tragedy is replicated in the deaths of the three actors, another example of Carter's interplay between theatre and life. Thus *'Exeunt omnes'* with Dora's wry comment: 'She'd always had a gift for exits' (p. 21). The matter-of-fact tone of Dora brings this interlude to a close. This punctuating of the story with **ironic** – at times sardonic – matter-of-fact comment is a feature of the tone and the structure of the story.

GLOSSARY

11	**Ruby Keeler** actress, singer, dancer; Hollywood star in the Warner musicals
12	**Miss Whiplash** ex-brothel owner (Lindi St Claire), presenting an image of a leather-clad dominatrix
14	**GBS** George Bernard Shaw (1856–1950), dramatist and theatre critic
16	**P. T. Barnum** American showman and tour manager and eventually, with J. A. Bailey, proprietor of the Barnum and Bailey Circus
17	**princes in the tower** nephews of Richard III, supposedly murdered by him in the Tower of London
	pink on the map the British Empire on maps was coloured pink; in the nineteenth century it covered much of the world
20	**the Great White Way** Broadway in New York, centre of the theatrical industry

PAGES 21–30

- The retelling of family history continues: Melchior and Peregrine, orphaned, are stranded in New York, but are taken in by an aunt.
- The different natures of the twins are explained.
- Perry's first disappearance and Melchior's eventual escape to London and the theatre are described.
- The conception of Dora and Nora and the death of their mother in childbirth are recounted.
- We learn of the early lives of the twins, adopted by Grandma Chance.

QUESTION
Leitmotifs are images or words that occur frequently in a work. They carry added significance. The cardboard crown passes to Melchior and becomes an integral part of the story. What significance does it have here and, more importantly, later in the story?

Melchior and Peregrine are left virtually destitute in New York, but survive on room service and charity from guests of the hotel until their strict Presbyterian aunt arrives from Scotland to take them 'home'. Peregrine escapes, a ten-year-old on the run, and vanishes for several years. Melchior returns with his aunt, having managed to hide the pasteboard crown that belonged to Ranulph, the father he worshipped. Forbidden to think of the stage, which is regarded by his aunt as sinful, Melchior eventually runs away to London. He finds a boarding house in Brixton and lives among theatrical performers of all varieties. Dora attempts to describe her conception, as Melchior makes love to Kitty, the seventeen-year-old servant. As war begins, the twins are born and Kitty dies in childbirth. Dora and Nora are immediately adopted by Mrs Chance. She becomes their grandma and gives them her name, Chance.

Grandma Chance's past is uncertain, but her establishment on the first day of the new century as a respectable landlady is described. She is a small, resilient lady with 'a rakish air' (p. 27), a creature of enduring habits; the strangest of these is that she wears no clothes in the house. Her refined tone covers a sharp and, at times, profane voice. Grandma's belief in the futility of war and her conviction that it is a conspiracy to kill off all the young men is set alongside her care for the twins when times are hard. The grandfather clock arrives, the only inheritance from the Presbyterian aunt. Melchior is unable to be contacted. Grandma Chance searches everywhere for him, finding him at last as the armistice is declared, playing Romeo in the West End. He denies parentage and Grandma accepts her charges. A knock at the door punctuates the story.

COMMENTARY

The disappearance of Peregrine from the clutches of the 'dour as hell' Presbyterian aunt has a touch of the mythical about it, not only in the ten-year-old vanishing 'clean away into America', but also in his mysterious survival through a series of 'doings and hoboings' to reappear years later 'as rich as Croesus' (p. 22). The deliberately sentimentalised portrait of the boy Melchior in the aunt's cold household, together with his escape, is pure fiction on Dora's part. You might consider why this is described in this manner. Melchior's escape from the aunt takes him, Dick Whittington-like, to London.

Another attempt by Dora to portray events that she can have had no experience of is the scene where Melchior fathers the twins. The versions of the conception in terms of lexis and sentence structure are worth analysing. The birth, too, is worth looking at in a similar way. Events that have come to Dora from Grandma Chance, so vivid that Dora believes she did see the seagull, add that touch of

CONTEXT

Dick Whittington was a pantomime character who set out for London to find his fortune after hearing that the streets were paved with gold and silver.

significant/insignificant detail. The idea that our memory is a construct of many experiences and received ideas causes the reader to question the whole issue of truth in a story. Typically in the midst of tragedy and pathos, there are moments of bawdy humour, the two faces of the theatre in life and in the novel.

The twins' adoption by Grandma Chance, another mysterious character, who seems to have almost invented herself and her subsequent family life, is integral to the story. She is also important thematically in the destruction of cultural stereotypes – particularly the father figure. Her appearance as if from nowhere (p. 26), appropriately on New Year's Day, is her new start and Dora does actually aver that 'Grandma invented this family' (p. 35). Apart from brief interludes when Perry resurfaces, Grandma Chance's household is entirely feminine. Her wry comment, when asked about never having had children of her own, is that she had 'never … known what men were *for*' until the moment she cuddled the twins for the first time (p. 28). Certainly Melchior's denial of responsibility, which immediately follows this in the text, provides a sharp contrast.

CONTEXT

One pervasive theme in *Wise Children* is family relationships. Fathers and their inability to accept responsibility is a recurrent issue, while the idea of inter-family sexual relationships occurs elsewhere, both imaginary and real.

GLOSSARY

21	**Shaftesbury Avenue** London street on which many theatres are found
	jism semen
22	**Presbyterian** Scottish Presbyterianism is often seen as a strict and joyless interpretation of scripture
	Croesus the last king of Lydia, in the sixth century BC, legendary for his wealth
25	***exigeante*** exacting, demanding
	Zeppelins German airships
26	**handle** cockney slang for name
27	**Electric Avenue** a street in Brixton, the first to be lit by electricity
	toque a small, close-fitting hat

PAGES 30–40

- Peregrine suddenly reappears into the lives of the young twins after years of absence in America.
- Peregrine supports the girls for some time, then disappears.
- Cyn, sent by Peregrine, becomes part of the Chance household.
- Mavis, her daughter, gives birth to Brenda, who in turn gives birth to Tiffany.
- There is further clarification of the Hazard family tree.
- Tristram becomes involved with Tiffany.

CONTEXT

Alaska is the largest state of the USA, in the far north-west of the American continent. Since 1867 it has belonged to America, although it did not become a state until January 1959. It was the scene of a gold rush in the early part of the twentieth century.

The caller at the door is greeted by Dora and Nora, who are naked apart from ribbons and identifiable as pirates only by eyepatch, scimitar and a skull and crossbones flag. This is the return of Uncle Peregrine from America, and the twins' first encounter with this romantic figure, whose first act is the conjuring of a pigeon from a pocket handkerchief. Peregrine offers several versions of his adventures in America: stories of fighting in Mexico, circus acts and gold rushes. However, Peregrine has called not just to visit the twins out of some sense of family duty, but to announce the impending marriage of Melchior to Lady Atalanta Lynde.

From this time Peregrine becomes the financial support for the twins, Grandma Chance having to be named their mother in the account books. The first of Perry's gifts is a phonograph. Peregrine pays for dancing lessons for the girls and provides a series of parcels, as well as magic tricks to entertain. As suddenly as he appeared, Peregrine is off again on his travels.

A visitor, a fourteen-year-old girl, appears with a scrap of paper as introduction from Peregrine. This is Cyn, who is taken in and who becomes eventually yet another strand of the complicated Chance family tree. Cyn bears several children, the eldest, Mavis, producing Brenda following a liaison with a GI, whom Dora and Nora then in turn take care of 'when she had *her* bit of trouble and brought home our precious little Tiffany' (p. 35). Brenda does eventually marry an ex-boxer and a strict Baptist. Tiffany is taught to dance by Dora and Nora at their grandly named Brixton Academy of Dance.

Tiffany pops in one day to Bard Road to find Dora and Nora entertaining Tristram – 'And no sooner did poor little Tiff set eyes on him than she fell' (p. 36). We discover that Tristram's twin brother, Gareth, has become a Jesuit missionary, and has not been seen or heard from for some ten years. This news comes from the Hazard family's 'Old Nanny', who is the source of much family gossip for Dora.

Dora offers some clarification for the complicated family tree, referring to characters we have already seen, and some we have yet to meet. Thus we learn that Melchior married Lady Atalanta (Wheelchair), secondly Delia Delaney (also known as Daisy Duck) from Hollywood, and thirdly the twenty-one-year-old best friend of Saskia. At the time she was playing Cordelia to his King Lear.

The third wife is instrumental in the move from stage into television advertising for the ageing Melchior and, occasionally, herself. Dora christens her 'My Lady Margarine'. Saskia and Imogen, acknowledged twin daughters of Sir Melchior, though in reality fathered by Peregrine, also take to television.

Further family gossip is revealed, including Tristram's expulsion from public school and his drink-driving crashes in expensive cars. While it is clearly love at first sight for Tiffany when she meets Tristram, he, in turn, is 'all of a dither' (p. 39), and takes her home with him, much to the dismay of Dora and Nora, who 'prepared themselves for heartbreak' (p. 40). When she visits them at Christmas, just a few months before their seventy-fifth birthday, Dora sees through the haggard and wan appearance of the once lovely Tiffany, who is now a hostess with Tristram on a tawdry television game show.

COMMENTARY

The veracity of Peregrine's account of his life in America is not the real issue. The clue lies in Dora's first words: 'Ooh, wasn't he a handsome young man in those days' and her admission that she might use 'the language of the pulp romance' in telling of his life and now his part in theirs (p. 30). Like many of the character sketches that introduce characters in the story, this one is worth analysing in terms of language, imagery and **allusions**. It is

? QUESTION Tiffany belongs to a different generation of showgirls to Dora and Nora, but there are some similarities. What are these similarities and what are the differences? Bear in mind that we have jumped a generation in a sense between music hall and television with the Hollywood years intervening.

CONTEXT

W. C. Fields (1880–1946) was an American comedian and actor, film star and accomplished juggler.

insignificant whether the allusions are true or false, though there are neat connections in the details, such as Perry's juggling and the link to W. C. Fields. Dora acknowledges the doubts with her italics in the phrase '*sole* confirmation' in reference to the events in Mexico (p. 32).

The description of the house with Perry in it has suggestions of family life, even the suggestion of what is as good as a marriage for Grandma Chance and Peregrine, though not one element is genuine. However, Peregrine, true to his name, is soon off on his travels, not before leaving another last gift for Grandma Chance, a fourteen-year-old waif on the doorstep, who is taken in without question. The theme of family is strongly stated in this section in what Grandma and Dora have to say. Cyn, the waif, becomes a part of the all-female family at Bard Road, this family created by Grandma Chance's 'sheer force of personality' (p. 35).

The idea of twins of different personalities is developed in the appearance of Tristram, twin to Gareth, the one a host of a trashy television game show, the other a Jesuit missionary. A further connection between Hazard and Chance lies in the fact that Tristram has become involved with Tiffany, daughter of Brenda and great-granddaughter of 'Our Cyn', and goddaughter to Nora and Dora. The complicated marital state of Melchior is virtually identical to that of his father – another of the mirror images to note.

The movement of the Hazard family, whose story began in Victorian theatre, encompasses the legitimate theatre, the music halls, film and now television. Television accounts for the irreverent name for the third Lady Hazard – 'My Lady Margarine' – and provides work for many of the family: Sir Melchior in advertising, Saskia as a television chef, Imogen as a goldfish in a children's show, Tristram as a game show host, and finally for Tiffany, albeit briefly, as his hostess. The appropriateness of roles in these various genres is worth considering here and at other points in the story.

See **Text 1** of **Extended commentaries** for further discussion of part of this section.

GLOSSARY

31	**flophouse** American slang for a cheap lodging house
33	**Bakelite** a brittle synthetic resin from which records were first made in the 1940s
36	**The rest is silence** Hamlet's last words just before he dies
	Jivaro a fierce Amazonian tribe of headhunters
38	**bête noire** someone especially disliked or seen as a threat
39	**Charleston** a lively dance of the early twentieth century

PAGES 40–52

- Tristram's television show is played on the video.
- Sir Melchior's birthday appearance on the show is interrupted by the appearance of Tiffany in a distressed state.
- Tristram is 'comforted' by Saskia.
- Brenda attacks Tristram.
- A girl's faceless body is found in the Thames.

QUESTION
The development of television in prolonging the careers of actors is worth considering at this point. Is there a difference between role play in theatre and role play on television?

Tristram's show with its catchphrase 'Lashings of Lolly!' is played on the video. It is intended as a special birthday tribute to his father, Sir Melchior. Tristram covers up Tiffany's absence on the show. The game is explained – a form of roulette in which money is double, tripled and so on – basically it is a show about greed. Suddenly Tiffany appears at the top of the staircase. She is dishevelled, wearing French knickers, purple stilettos and a grotesque American football shirt with a giant 69 in the centre. There is a wallflower in her hair and she is carrying flowers. She is singing unintelligibly.

While Nora and Wheelchair are weeping, Dora realises that Tiffany is pregnant. Nora presses the standby button, during which pause Tristram reveals that he cannot take the responsibility of fatherhood.

The return to the video reveals Tiffany with feet bleeding approaching Tristram and Sir Melchior. She offers Tristram a wallflower and then thrusts the rest of her spray at him apart from a single daffodil. Again she sings a nonsense verse before switching to a vulgar song about whores. She rips off her shirt, but Sir Melchior covers her naked breasts with a mink stole. His wife (My Lady Margarine) declares that they had wanted Tristram to marry her. However, Tiffany breaks from her daze. She calls out in a ringing voice for a cab, turns to the camera and offers her professional smile and then takes her leave. Tristram comes to himself and bids goodnight to the audience as if nothing has happened.

The search for Tiffany has been going on for some time, but Tristram passed out after the show and was comforted by an unnamed female. The single red hair that Nora plucks from his lapel is evidence enough. It belongs to Saskia, his older half-sister.

Brenda, Tiffany's mother, appears, white with rage. Then comes news that a young girl's unidentified body has been found in the river. Wheelchair goes to her room to play on her gramophone the song 'Eurydice'. Nora and Dora fortify the tea with rum and wonder if the party will be cancelled, but decide that it will go ahead as Tiffany was only a peripheral part of the family. There is even a sense of relish that it will be worth attending.

COMMENTARY

The reactions of Dora, Nora and Wheelchair to the opening of Tristram's show are apparent, especially in the choice of language and tone. There are a number of 'voices' in this phase of the story – Nora, Wheelchair, Tristram's two voices, and the overall **narrative voice** and commentary of Dora.

The appearance of Tiffany is excruciating, made more poignant by virtue of it going out live on television. Her similarities to Ophelia are numerous – her betrayal by Tristram, her physical appearance, state of mind, the singing, her actions, and ultimately her apparent death by drowning. This is the moment when the idea of life imitating art is most sharply developed, though it has occurred in previous generations of the Hazard story.

The aftermath of the television show reveals another secret in the Hazard family's 'bulging closetful of skeletons' in the relationship between Tristram and his half-sister Saskia (p. 48). The contrast between the Hazard and Chance families is dramatised in the appearance of Brenda. The Chance household's compassion is clear. This is even amusingly portrayed in the midst of tragedy. The 'whoosh of rubber tyres' from Wheelchair (another of those occasions when Wheelchair is described in mechanical rather than human terms) is even more poignant (p. 50).

The sadness of the moment is set against the conflicting thoughts and emotions as the chapter comes to an end – malice towards Saskia, dismay at the failure of the morning's promise, a half-hearted suggestion of blackmail and then a reiteration of the motto 'Life must go on' with even a note of triumphant glee that the party will be well worth attending. Note that these emotions rise on a scale and that the final one anticipates with relish what might happen. The final comments reiterate the life force of Nora and Dora's philosophy.

> **CONTEXT**
>
> The juxtaposition of the tragic with the potentially comic is a recurrent **motif** both in *Wise Children* and in the plays of Shakespeare, notably in the tragedies, but also in the darker comedies. There are later direct references in *Wise Children* to the tragic and comic aspects of life and drama.

GLOSSARY	
49	Evelyn Laye (1900–96) actress and musical comedy star married to Sonnie Hale, who left her for Jessie Matthews
51	forsythia a shrub with yellow flowers in the spring

CHAPTER 2

PAGES 53–61

- Dora and Nora's dancing lessons when they are six are described.
- Their first visit to the theatre determines the girls' careers as dancers.
- They see their father for the first time from a distance.
- There are retrospective reflections on the girls' careers in song and dance.
- The girls' first night on stage and the return of Uncle Peregrine from his travels to see it are recounted.

At the age of six Dora and Nora attend dancing classes, travelling by tram across London from Brixton to Clapham. For their seventh birthday treat they are taken by Grandma Chance to see Fred and Adèle Astaire in *Lady Be Good*. Tea complete with cucumber sandwiches on a tray is served in the interval. Suddenly Grandma points to the dress circle at a handsome young man and a blonde lady. As the lights dim for the second half, Grandma announces to the twins that the man is their father. However, in the crush leaving the theatre their father disappears, much to Grandma's chagrin.

The girls are curious about fathers and Grandma gives them a rudimentary sex education on their way home. From this moment, their curiosity about and fascination for their father with his glamour in the theatre and the press are aroused. The excitement of the day is complete when a toy theatre from Peregrine arrives. The birthday, sixty-eight years ago, provokes memories of the stage career of the song and dance girls in vaudeville (variety shows), degenerating eventually into nude revues.

Back to their childhood now, the dancing lessons continue, until finally the girls appear as little brown birds in the pantomime *Babes in the Wood*. Their debut is attended by Grandma Chance and Our Cyn, but their pleasure is complete when Peregrine unexpectedly returns from his travels to congratulate them.

COMMENTARY

This section illustrates Carter's ability to evoke atmosphere of time and place. She builds up images appealing to the senses, typically adjectives and similes which add to the richness of the text. We have the recreation of the tram journey across London (pp. 53–4), the dancing class (pp. 53–4), the splendour of a first theatre visit (pp. 54–5), the excitement of a seventh birthday celebration (pp. 54–8) and the atmosphere of pantomime, on and off stage (p. 61). Interspersing this we have a flash forward in time (flashback, if we take Dora's **narrative** position as the seventy-five-year-old) to the tawdriness of theatrical lodgings (p. 59).

CONTEXT

All five senses are evoked in the images, both pleasant and not so pleasant, used to describe their seventh birthday celebrations. Carter's use of simile here has many effects – comic, associative, **anticlimactic** and **bathetic**.

Often there is a sharp contrast between the superficial aspects and the realities of life. Two examples serve to illustrate how this technique works throughout the narrative. A close contrast occurs when the beauty and pleasure of the antique Venetian toy theatre is replaced by the reality of Brenda's 'bit of trouble', Tiffany, who needed to be 'kept ... in disposables until she learned to piss in a pot' (p. 58). The lexical choices accentuate the contrast. An image which spans the years is the wonder of their first visit to the theatre with its mock splendour (plaster cherubs, gilt swags, crystal candelabra, red plush), which contrasts with the twins' visit on a rainy Sunday to a seedy, leaking north London cinema to see themselves years later in the Hollywood film *A Midsummer Night's Dream* (Chapter 3, p. 110).

Further descents from the serious to the comic, the sublime to the most basic, are seen, for example when Dora describes Miss Worthington's 'droopy tutu' (p. 53), and compares Nora's 'bum' when they do their exercises to 'two hard-boiled eggs in a handkerchief' (p. 54).

Carter's demythologising of fairy tales is apparent in the use of 'once upon a time' three times in the early parts of this chapter. The phrase also serves to remind us of the decades that have passed. A brief résumé of the twins' life in theatre takes us quickly through the years from pantomime to theatre, music hall, film, vaudeville, **burlesque** and finally to nude revues. The phrase draws our attention to the fairy-tale elements that appear in the fabric of the story, either by **allusions** or by phrases worked into the fabric of the text.

The portrayal of Grandma Chance spreads across the non-chronological narrative, but here we have a number of characteristics which show her various qualities. The portrayal is affectionate – 'What we knew for certain was, our grandma loved us' (p. 57) – and comic: 'we knew she looked a bit of a funniosity' (p. 55). Her attempts at refinement are shown in little details like the crooked finger or the voice – 'a nayce musical comedy' (p. 55) – or her disapproval of Jessie Matthews, judged 'common' by many

> **CONTEXT**
>
> In a Noël Coward song, Mrs Worthington is advised: 'Don't put your daughter on the stage'.

> **❓ QUESTION**
>
> Carter in 'Notes from the Front Line' claimed to be in the 'demythologising business' (in *On Gender and Writing*, edited by Michelene Wandor, 1983). What do you think she meant by this? To what myths might she be referring?

> **CONTEXT**
>
> Jessie Matthews (1907–81) was a star of the theatre and film, nicknamed the Dancing Divinity. She was named in the divorce of Sonnie Hale.

? **QUESTION**
In what ways does Dora resemble Grandma Chance? In what ways are the two different?

at the time as she had been involved in divorce proceedings. The swoop from the elegant is often qualified, here in the verb and the simile: 'spitting out her famous vowels like cherrystones' (p. 59). Moreover, incidents of refinement are often punctuated by a final descent into amusing vulgarity of language or behaviour. The belch, the challenging glare and the demand 'Who let that out?' typify her defiance of convention, already seen in her nude housework, her vegetarianism and her attitude to men, particularly old men, who send young men to war.

Peregrine now features more in the story, his sudden, almost magical appearances characterising this larger than life figure. A kind of surrogate father, he arrives bearing wonderful gifts, endearing him to the girls and to Grandma Chance. However, he frequently disappears as theatrically as he has appeared. It is important to remember that the portrayal of characters comes through the perceptions and sensibilities of Dora, the narrator. The 'I' and the 'eye' of an autobiographical tale qualify the accuracy of portrayal of events and characters.

GLOSSARY	
53	**liberty bodices** short undergarments like vests
	fouetté a ballet step on one foot
55	**Damascus road** a conversion, a sudden change in lifestyle; the biblical conversion of St Paul took place on the road to Damascus
58	**Harlequin, Columbine, Pantaloon** comic characters from *commedia dell'arte*, the first a foolish lover of Columbine, a servant girl; the last a lecherous old man
59	**Archie Rice** middle-aged, third-rate comedian and song and dance man, played by Laurence Olivier in John Osborne's *The Entertainer*
61	**Jeyes Fluid** a powerful disinfectant

PAGES 61–75

- Peregrine escorts the family to Brighton.
- He takes them to a Pierrot show and the comedy act of Gorgeous George is described.
- Melchior Hazard is playing Macbeth. Peregrine takes the girls backstage to meet their father, but he ignores them.
- Twins Saskia and Imogen are born.
- Peregrine loses his money in the Wall Street Crash and leaves for America and the movies.

CONTEXT

The Wall Street Crash was the name given to the financial collapse of October 1929, when fortunes were lost on the New York Stock Exchange. It was a major factor in the early stages of the Depression. As a result, many investors became bankrupt and there were numerous suicides from high-rise buildings on Wall Street.

Uncle Perry suddenly reappears and whisks the family off in a taxi for a day out to Brighton. A lavish picnic on the beach is followed by a matinée performance on the pier. Dora looks back on her thirteen-year-old self and recalls the happiness of that outing – 'When I think of happiness, I always think of Brighton' – even though they 'did the heights and depths, that day' (p. 63).

The star of the Pierrot show is Gorgeous George, whose performance involves risqué jokes, double entendre and audience participation. The climax of his act is a sentimental and patriotic finale, the culmination of which involves his stripping off to reveal a map of the world. With the singing of 'Land of Hope and Glory' and 'Rule, Britannia' and cries of 'long live the King', the show is brought to an end (pp. 66–7).

The excitement of an impromptu dance performance by the girls in the street, accompanied by an uncertain memory of Perry with a harmonica or a 'Lovely little band' of musicians, is recalled by Dora (p. 68).

The enjoyment of the day is clouded somewhat when Perry, having noticed a poster advertising Melchior Hazard in *Macbeth*, reminds the girls that Melchior is their father. Perry takes the girls backstage to Melchior's dressing room. Melchior greets Peregrine but totally ignores the girls, referring to them as 'your lovely daughters' (p. 72). Devastated, the girls are comforted by Peregrine, and Peregrine reminds his brother of the gypsy's warning about wise children and wise fathers.

The day ends with the return to London, the cab driver having made a romantic hit with Cyn. Perry is dropped off at Eaton Square in front of an elegant house. The story suddenly jumps to a recollection of the twin sisters Saskia and Imogen, the so-called legitimate generation.

There is a further leap forward in time to when the girls are earning wages in provincial theatre as dancers. Peregrine, having lost all his money in the Wall Street Crash, leaves for America.

COMMENTARY

We move forward six years to an eventful day. Peregrine appears once again out of nowhere. Look closely at the lexical choices and the structure of the sentences in the opening paragraph (p. 62). This jolly abruptness, a larger than life quality about him, is picked up each time he appears. It pervades this memorable day out in Brighton, which begins appropriately enough with magic and illusion, but ends with reality and disillusion for the twins (Dora says: 'We went from the ridiculous to the sublime, and broke our hearts, as well').

The magic of the picnic is partly credible, partly beyond belief. The idea of **magic realism** (see **Magic realism**) has featured strongly in Carter's work, and here in a novel quite rooted in the realities of life we see the feature emerge in Dora's **narrative**. Hard-boiled eggs from noses and coffee poured from the cabby's hat are possible, but the magical disappearance of the picnic goes beyond Perry being a 'marvellous conjurer' (p. 62).

Perry's size is stressed (here he is the size of a polar bear), and he seems to grow in stature each time he appears. Colour (his red hair and his startling clothes), his distinctive smell of cologne, his speech and his extravagant actions add to the effect of a larger than life figure.

The smell of cologne provokes a recollection of a dreadful and delightful thought that, later on, during the war, Perry had actually

CONTEXT

'Perry picked hard-boiled eggs out of our noses' (p. 62): this is the first of several references to Peregrine's conjuring tricks in this episode. His theatrical knack for conjuring and illusion does not fade, but continues intermittently right up to his producing of Tiffany from the trunk and the twins from his pockets in Chapter 5. Some tricks are credible, while others seem to be touched by magic, adding to the layers of illusion and magic found throughout the work. Harry Houdini (1874–1926), the famous magician, pioneered a variety of escape acts in the late nineteenth and early twentieth centuries.

made love to Dora. It turns out to be another man, dismissed casually as 'that Free Pole' (p. 63). Perhaps this short phrase says much about Dora's attitude to love and life. However, this thought introduces a theme that runs through the story: that of incestuous relationships, real, imaginary or vicarious.

Carter recreates the atmosphere of the show on the pier, again with many appeals to the senses. The act of Gorgeous George is typical of the time, typical indeed of a number of music hall comedians. The double entendre, the audience participation and the patriotism belong to many in that era of show business, but the map of the world tattooed on his body quite literally marks George out from the rest. He strips down to a Union Jack G-string (the subject of amused, vulgar asides by Dora), and to the tune of 'Rule, Britannia' he reveals an 'enormous statement' in the pink of the British Empire. Dora is reminded of her otherness, 'offspring of the bastard king' (p. 67). George resurfaces at two later points in the novel, these appearances contrasting sharply with this pre-war performance.

The memory of dancing in the streets after they have left the theatre enables Dora to comment on the accuracy of memory or the magic realism of what happened. The fisherman on the pier with a mackerel that might have been a tin can causes Dora to say 'I misremember' (p. 68). However, we have the magic narrative of the moment as they dance and Perry plays a harmonica, which seems to turn into a band of quite specific detail – 'four Black gentlemen in suits and straw hats, trumpet, trombone, clarinet, percussion' (p. 68) – that, like Perry's picnic, disappears suddenly. An earlier generation had taken part in impromptu street theatre, Estella and Peregrine performing in Sydney (Chapter 1, p. 18), another of the incidents in which the Hazard family history is mirrored.

The **irony** of the song chosen by the girls, 'Is You Is or Is You Ain't My Baby', serves here to introduce a musical **motif** that appears at different points. However, along with a poster advertising 'Melchior Hazard and Company' in *Macbeth*, it provokes Perry into telling the girls what they already know: that Melchior, not he, is their father. The trepidation of what Perry is

CHECK THE BOOK
For a detailed analysis of Gorgeous George's comedy, see pp. 285–6 of Kate Webb's essay 'Seriously Funny: *Wise Children*', in *Flesh and the Mirror: Essays on the Art of Angela Carter* (edited by Lorna Sage).

CHECK THE BOOK
'Magic realist novels and stories have, typically, a strong narrative drive, in which the recognizably realistic mingles with the unexpected and the inexplicable, and in which elements of dreams, fairy story, or mythology combine with the everyday, often in a mosaic or kaleidoscopic pattern of refraction and recurrence.' For a brief introduction to magic realism, see *The Oxford Companion to English Literature* (sixth edition, edited by Margaret Drabble).

about to do causes mixed feelings in Dora, whose longing to see her father is glamorised in her language (p. 70). This language has romantic, even explicitly sexual connotations (p. 72) as Dora anticipates meeting Melchior, who is, after all, her father.

The pathos of the portrayal of the two girls on the outside is accentuated by the reception they receive – or rather do not. Melchior literally overlooks them, greets Peregrine in a patronising manner – 'how nice of you to come and visit me' – and refers to the girls as 'your lovely daughters' (p. 72).

The memory of Perry rescuing them in magical fashion, part of which account Dora admits to knowing 'cannot be a true one', contains hidden elements of truth as to what exactly happens at this point. Peregrine's warning embodies the title of the novel and serves as one of the many mottoes in the book; indeed, it is the most significant of them all: 'It's a wise child that knows its own father ... But wiser yet the father who knows his own child' (p. 73).

The **anticlimax** of the day draws to a close. A seemingly insignificant incident, Perry being dropped off back in London at Eaton Square, is put into perspective by Dora's comment 'naughty boy', for she knows the address (p. 73). We then have Grandma's calculations when Saskia and Imogen, the daughters of Melchior and Lady Atalanta, are born in May (do we too recall that August bank holiday nine months earlier?). Finally, we have a third clue: Perry's sadness when he sees the Hazard twins wheeled out in their baby carriage. Carter draws the reader into the puzzle of Hazard family history on several other similar occasions.

Peregrine's disappearance is, in one way, uncharacteristic. Having lost all his money in the Wall Street Crash, crumpets replace the extravagant chocolates. Hazard and Chance have dealt him a blow. However, there is a hint of the future in his idea of going into the movies when he returns to Los Angeles.

CONTEXT

Carter uses the idea of wise children elsewhere. Her favourite story in her edited collection *The Virago Book of Fairy Tales* was the one in which the heroine provides for the tsar the impossible 'without batting an eyelid'. The phrase also occurs in *Nights at the Circus* and *The Bloody Chamber*.

GLOSSARY

63	**hokey-pokey man** magician or conjuror
	subfusc drab, dull, dark
	Evening in Paris and Ashes of Violets common perfumes of the period
64	**'fraizy crazy'** strawberry coloured, from the French for strawberry, *fraise*
68	**Black Bottom** popular 1920s dance, regarded as risqué
69	**Birnam Wood ... Dunsinane** as *Macbeth* draws to a close, Birnam Wood, in reality camouflaged soldiers, appears to move towards Dunsinane
74	**Cecil Beaton** (1904–80) fashion and portrait photographer
75	**moolah** slang for money

PAGES 75–95

- Dora and Nora's stage career begins.
- The death of Grandma Chance in the Blitz is described in a future recollection.
- Nora's love life and Dora's first affair are described.
- Peregrine returns.
- The girls feature in a revue starring Melchior, and written by Peregrine.
- The girls enjoy the benefits of success.

Dora and Nora begin their stage career in pantomime in Kennington. One afternoon, Lady Atalanta Hazard appears with her two children and their nanny to watch the afternoon show. She recognises the twins and later sends forget-me-nots. Saskia and Imogen react in appropriately different ways: the first howls to gain attention; the second sleeps with her mouth wide open.

After the panto season Dora and Nora take to the circuit of provincial theatres. They dye their hair black and call themselves 'The Lucky Chances' (p. 80). The scrapbooks and programmes are kept by Grandma Chance right up until her death in 1944. She dies in an air raid on her way to the off-licence for beer.

CONTEXT

Angela Carter frequently works Shakespearian phrases into the fabric of the text. Here Dora's recollection that they would sneak off to watch Melchior 'strut and fret his hour upon the stage' is, appropriately, from *Macbeth*. 'Darling buds of May' (p. 74) is another Shakespeare phrase, this one from Sonnet 18, 'Shall I compare thee to a summer's day?', which has worked itself into the English language. H. E. Bates used it as the title for his first of five books about the Larkin family, which in turn became a popular television series in the early 1990s.

Accounts of Nora's more outgoing nature with men start with her first affair in a theatre alley with the pantomime goose from *Mother Goose*, a much older man. Dora pretends to be Nora in order to keep her sister's affair hidden from the goose's wife. Unbeknown to Dora, Nora becomes pregnant; and later, on stage in Nottingham, she loses the baby. There is no further contact from the goose. Nora bounces back and falls for the drummer in the theatre band.

The girls start to progress in their career. The 'aged drummer' is soon replaced by a young tenor in Nora's affections (p. 82). Dora herself falls for the boy and asks Nora to give him to her as a birthday present. Changing perfumes, the girls impersonate each other and Dora receives her present: one night of passion with her sister's boyfriend. Nora manages to keep up the disguise for some time that night, but after a few drinks her outgoing nature surfaces. Fortunately for Dora, 'by the time Nora started dancing on the table' the majority of the party are drunk themselves, 'so nobody noticed she was behaving out of character' (p. 84). Nora then leaves with the pianist, still pretending to be Dora.

Melchior Hazard and Lady Atalanta appear at their birthday celebrations. Dora dances with her father, who still does not acknowledge paternity. He kisses Dora. His birthday presents for the two girls are parts in his new London revue *What You Will*. Dora returns to tell Grandma Chance the news and finds that Peregrine has returned.

The music for the revue has been written by Mr Piano Man, Dora's new love – thanks to Nora's night with him while pretending to be her sister. The revue has been written by Peregrine and stars Melchior, by now a great man of the theatre. The girls sing and dance in various Shakespearian sketches. Success brings its rewards. Nora has a succession of affairs, and Mr Piano Man buys Dora a fur coat. Peregrine and Grandma Chance enjoy each other's company, as the girls enjoy a rich social life. In retrospect, Dora ponders her relationship with Grandma Chance, and considers the real girls beneath the image presented by her and her sister at the time.

CONTEXT

What You Will is the subtitle of Shakespeare's play *Twelfth Night*; here it is also, as the title of Melchior and Peregrine's revue, a play on William Shakespeare's name.

COMMENTARY

The identity of the girls is recognised by Lady Atalanta (destined to be Wheelchair). An **ironic**, anonymous gift of flowers, forget-me-nots, is possible acknowledgement of this, though, in fact, later the girls do not forget her. Despite her appearances in the early parts of Dora's story being heralded by the sheep **motif**, Lady Atalanta is sympathetically portrayed throughout. The descriptions of her daughters, Saskia and Imogen, are decidedly barbed; even at this stage the jealousy of the former and the dopiness of the latter are apparent.

Dora's **narrative** is filled out with other **voices**, the Hazard family nanny here acknowledged as a source of information (p. 76). This method enables background details to be added to Dora's archives of memory. A similar recollection, this one by Peregrine, has already been referred to in another context (Chapter 1, p. 18). The first-person narrative contains many voices, some dramatised by Dora's recreation of events, some acknowledged as sources of information beyond Dora's experience, and others which surface in more subtle narrative shifts.

The death of Grandma Chance, on her way to the off-licence in the middle of the Blitz, is described, though she will resurface in the narrative as Dora's recollections move back and forth in time. Her death has that double touch of tragedy and comedy, emerging in Dora's affectionate, comic and sad detail (p. 79).

The life of the theatre, on and off stage, is of course central to the story. This section traces the progress of the twins from pantomime in Kennington (p. 75) to life on the road at fifteen (p. 77), to dyed hair and the stage name 'The Lucky Chances' at sixteen (p. 80). The discovery of the programmes kept by Grandma has a touch of pathos. Dora sees 'the whole of our lives' stored away in a trunk in the loft (p. 78). The paper has now turned to 'brown dust, like the dust of bones', a sharp memento mori (a reminder of death).

Carter comically explores the growing sexual awareness and exploits of the girls, though it seems to be Nora who is the more promiscuous. Her first affair with the pantomime goose has a

CONTEXT

The Blitz was the name given to the intensive German air raids on Britain in 1940 and 1941 which resulted in the destruction of many buildings and the death of over fifteen thousand people. The name derives from the German word 'blitzkrieg', meaning 'lightning war'.

? QUESTION
How does
the affair between
Nora and the
pantomime goose
(pp. 80–1) contrast
with Dora's first
affair (pp. 83–6)?
What can their
individual
attitudes towards
love and sex tell
us about their
different
characters?

CONTEXT
Throughout *Wise
Children* the
language used to
describe Melchior
not only reveals
aspects of his
appearance and
character, but also
illuminates Dora's
mixed feelings
towards him.

pantomimic quality and a shabbiness (pp. 80–1), but this is placed into a different context by Dora's advice to the reader: 'Don't run away with the idea that it was a squalid, furtive, miserable thing'; Nora 'had a passion to know about Life, all its dirty corners' (p. 81).

The mistaken identities, impersonations, role play – particularly playing on the identical appearance of twins – of the story are Shakespearian in their comic and dramatic effects. Dora's deception of the goose's wife in masquerading as Nora is the first of many such deceits. A reversal of the masquerade occurs shortly after the goose incident, when Dora is attracted to the boyfriend of her twin sister. The sharing of the boyfriend as Dora's birthday present from her sister is described in explicit and tender detail (pp. 85–6). The metaphor of the lilac decaying is repeated later in the story (Chapter 5, p. 225), one of the many recurrent motifs in Carter's rich prose.

The sudden appearance of Melchior is described in romantic terms. Dora admits that her 'heart went pit-a-pat' when they dance, her father 'romantically garbed in evening dress' (pp. 86–7). His kiss and his present, roles for the girls in his West End Shakespearian revue, complete another memorable day. The early-morning walk alone through Brixton adds touches of realistic detail. The reader is made aware that Peregrine has returned through the recognisable detail of Grandma finishing off a freshly opened bottle of crème de menthe. Indeed, the events of the memorable night just experienced are topped by his sudden reappearance, described once again in larger than life terms in a short paragraph crammed with familiar detail (p. 88).

Coincidence, whether it be dramatic device or realistic phenomenon, brings together Peregrine, the writer of the revue; Melchior, its star; Nora and Dora, singing and dancing in sketches; and Mr Piano Man. The attachment between Mr Piano Man and Dora encapsulates some of the thematic strands in the novel: mistaken identity (to the end he thinks the real Dora is the Dora – actually Nora – he first dated on the night of their party); the sending of lilac; the lack of sentiment of Nora and Dora in the affair; finally the end of the affair placed in the wider context of time (his forgotten hits, his 'Missing in action' in 1942, Dora's visits to his mother with the small details of coincidence and sentiment).

The rise in fortunes of the Chance family is described in a series of incidents in fashionable nightclubs, restaurants and hotels. The detail captures the spirit of the times, though typically the extravagance is qualified by humour, by Grandma Chance's comic refinements, idiosyncrasies or her bluntness. Dora's later realisation of the illusion and the irony of it all runs through this year of grace.

CONTEXT

There are many examples of chance and coincidence in *Wise Children*, both major and minor. The names Hazard and Chance are almost synonymous. The two forces, hazard and chance, play a significant part in many plays, especially Shakespeare's, as well as in Carter's novel.

GLOSSARY

78	**ENSA** Entertainment National Service Association, providing entertainment for Second World War troops
	Burma Road route from Burma into China used by the Allies during the Second World War
79	**VE-day** day marking the Allied victory in Europe: 8 May 1945
81	**Green Room** backstage room in a theatre for resting
	Chu Chin Chow popular show, based on the *Arabian Nights* story of Ali Baba and the forty thieves
83	**Epps' cocoa** the advertisement for Epps' cocoa featured two smiling, innocent-looking children
90	**John Martin** (1789–1854) English Romantic painter
	V and A the Victoria and Albert Museum in London

PAGES 95–109

- The eighteen-year-old girls are invited to the Lynde Court Twelfth Night Costume Ball.
- Dora meets her first lover again, who still believes she is Nora.
- As they are upstairs, fire breaks out.
- The house burns, but the guests continue the revels out of doors.
- Peregrine rescues Nora and Melchior's cardboard crown from the fire.
- The American producer announces plans for the company to perform in Hollywood.

Melchior's success allows him to indulge in elaborate decoration at Lynde Court, the estate inherited by Lady Atalanta. The success of *What You Will* is to be celebrated by a Twelfth Night Costume Ball. Dora and Nora are 'bidden' rather than invited to attend (p. 96). The girls are informed that Hollywood film directors will be present and the party is a type of audition.

At the ball the Shakespearian costumes and trappings are elaborate. Nora engages in conversation with a little, bald, fat man who is smoking a cigar. Dora meets the young tenor, her first love (and Nora's ex), who is working as a waiter. He still believes that Dora is Nora. While Nora is dancing with the fat man, who has put down his cigar, Dora and the young boy kiss under the table and then escape to the master bedroom. Their lovemaking is disturbed by a call of 'Fire!' (p. 100).

Dora and the boy escape the flames by climbing out of the window and down the ivy; they continue their lovemaking in the shrubbery. When they finally emerge, they can find no sign of either Nora or Peregrine. The fire seems to have 'unleashed a kind of madness' (p. 103). Various Shakespearian characters are indulging in sexual activities; Dora spots her second lover Mr Piano Man with a minor actress. Dora runs around the wild scene, seeking Nora. She meets Melchior, who has rescued a huge carved chair. Calling for champagne, he sits and watches his house burn. As Dora mourns the loss of her sister, Melchior laments the loss of his crown. Suddenly out of the flames Peregrine emerges, Nora in his arms, the cardboard crown on his head.

The circumstances of the fire are explained. The cigar of the fat man with Nora set fire to the tablecloth. The fire went unnoticed, as the waiter had disappeared upstairs with a female guest. As the film producer announces that he is taking the cast of the revue to Hollywood, Melchior and Peregrine argue over the cardboard crown. Hearing the words 'additional dialogue by William Shakespeare!' from the producer, Peregrine loses interest in the argument and tosses the crown to Melchior (p. 108). Peregrine takes Dora and Nora home, and gives a lift to their boyfriend. This is the last Dora sees of the tenor.

CHECK THE FILM
Max Reinhardt's glamorous Hollywood film of *A Midsummer Night's Dream*, starring teenager Mickey Rooney as Puck and James Cagney as Bottom, was made in 1935. The film features the screenwriting credit: 'Dialogue by William Shakespeare'.

COMMENTARY

This central incident exemplifies the **carnivalesque** features of Carter's style. The Twelfth Night celebrations are no coincidence, its revels belonging traditionally to the idea of carnival (see **Carnival and carnivalesque**).

The pretentiousness of Melchior's role as the head of the 'Royal Family of the British Theatre' (p. 95) is seen in the country house. The extravagances of the decor are clear, Perry's understated, **ironic** comment about 'marginally too august a setting' voicing the reader's reaction (p. 96). The costume ball, the musical entrance, the buffet crowned by a stuffed swan – all these add to an atmosphere of excess. These provide the backdrop for the even greater excesses that follow, as normal order is thrown on its head.

Dora's meeting with her first love, the young boy, results in their making love in the master bedroom, recognisable at once by the glass case containing the cardboard crown. This incident of lovemaking in Melchior's inner sanctum is replicated years later at another celebration (Chapter 5, pp. 219–22). The masquerade of identity is preserved; the young boy notices the different scent, but smells burning just at the moment when Dora might have revealed her true identity.

At this point the carnivalesque elements run riot, and the reader is confronted by sexual exploits in the shrubbery; Saskia gorging herself on the swan from the banquet; chorus girls throwing champagne on the fire; chorus boys urinating on the fire; and Melchior self-aggrandisingly sitting in a huge carved chair in front of the blazing mansion and calling for champagne (pp. 101–7). The sheer excess of images and language provides 'an orgiastic aspect to this night of disaster'. The idea of 'guests at a masquerade who've all gone suddenly to hell' sums up this carnivalesque, topsy-turvy world (p. 103). Most ludicrous of all, in the face of the loss of the mansion and the possible loss of one of his daughters, is Melchior's lamentation over his lost cardboard crown. His final valuing of the crown – 'More than wealth, or fame, or women, or children' (p. 105) – causes Dora not to berate him, but to almost applaud the Shakespearian performance. The **melodramatic** emergence of Peregrine from the flames carrying Nora in his arms is literally capped by the crown on his head.

CONTEXT

Twelfth Night occurs on 5 January, marking the end of the Christmas festivities. In earlier times a cake was baked containing a bean and small silver coins. Whoever received the piece containing the bean became the bean king or the Lord of Misrule. This person was responsible for the evening's revels, in which all kinds of outrageous behaviour irrespective of status or authority was allowed.

QUESTION
The celebrations at the manor house (pp. 100–7) display a number of the qualities of carnival in its original sense. How does Carter exemplify the essence of carnival behaviour in this scene?

The confusion of identity regarding Nora/Dora is resolved by Nora, like Lady Macbeth in a crisis, fainting. The Shakespearian note is continued as Melchior becomes Richard III, calling out for his crown. As he holds the crown out of his brother's reach, Peregrine seems to grow larger – the growth emphasised in three comparatives: 'bigger, taller, wider' (p. 107). The fact that this perception comes from Dora is significant. The petty game is brought to an **anticlimactic** end, as Perry, having lost interest, tosses the crown to the wailing Melchior.

However, preceding this anticlimax is the announcement that the cigar-smoking producer will take the production of *What You Will* to America. The irony of his reference to the two brothers as geniuses is lost in the bemused applause of the crowd and Peregrine's inaccurate prediction that it will be 'A dream come true!' (p. 108).

See **Text 2** of **Extended commentaries** for further discussion of part of this section.

GLOSSARY		
97	**MGM** Metro-Goldwyn-Mayer, the huge American film studio of the mid twentieth century	
98	**Bristol glass** a semi-opaque or opalescent decorative glass made in the Bristol area	
100	**Samson and Delilah, Judith and Holofernes** in the Bible Delilah deprived Samson of his strength by cutting off his hair; Judith decapitated the Assyrian general Holofernes	

CHAPTER 3

PAGES 110–24

- Shortly before their seventy-fifth birthday, Dora and Nora visit a shabby cinema to see themselves in *A Midsummer Night's Dream*.
- Back in the past, the girls travel to America for the filming of *A Midsummer Night's Dream*.
- In New York Peregrine introduces them to Daisy Duck.
- From New York they cross America by train to Hollywood.
- Nora falls in love again and Dora meets Irish.

Almost back in the present, Dora and Nora visit a shabby cinema in Notting Hill which is showing the film they made years ago in Hollywood. The cinema is run-down, leaking and virtually empty. Two men are engaged in oral sex, which amuses and enlivens Dora. After the film, one of the men approaches the twins in the street and asks if they are the Chance sisters. Nora wonders why the film is described as a 'masterpiece of kitsch' (p. 111).

Over a gin, Dora recalls the days leading up to the filming of *A Midsummer Night's Dream*. The twins arrive in New York to be greeted by a flurry of cameras – Dora says it felt as if they 'trembled on the brink of stardom', and they 'even featured in the *Pathé News*' (p. 113). They bring with them a casket of earth from Stratford-upon-Avon which Melchior intends to sprinkle ceremonially on the set of the film.

CONTEXT
The Pathé group produced newsreels for the cinema in the days before television was popular.

Peregrine is in New York to welcome them. He takes them to a lavish apartment overlooking Central Park which belongs to Hollywood star Delia Delaney, real name Daisy Duck. She and Peregrine are romantically involved.

The following morning Peregrine takes Dora to a construction site: the site of the Plaza theatre, where his father, their grandfather, had killed his wife and her lover during their playing of Othello, Desdemona and Iago.

The next stage is the journey across the United States. Nora falls in love with Tony, a young Italian from Little Italy in New York hoping to make his name in Hollywood. Peregrine introduces Dora to Irish, real name Ross O'Flaherty, an older man with whom she begins a relationship. He is a writer, who later will portray Dora unflatteringly in his **memoirs**, and a heavy drinker. He becomes Dora's lover and teacher of literature.

CONTEXT
The area of New York where Italian families settled in the early part of the twentieth century was known as Little Italy.

COMMENTARY

Dora's **voice** again is characterised by a blend of close observation, straight **narrative** with serious comment and colloquialisms. Sentences with the subject omitted, exclamations, direct addresses to the reader, inconsequential musings and the south London vocabulary contribute to the chatty style.

CONTEXT

According to the legend, the vampire Dracula must lie in soil from his graveyard during daylight hours.

 CHECK THE BOOK

In her illuminating essay 'Seriously Funny: *Wise Children*' Kate Webb identifies several real-life stars referred to in the novel (in *Flesh and the Mirror: Essays on the Art of Angela Carter*, edited by Lorna Sage).

CONTEXT

Marcel Proust (1871–1922) was a French novelist whose *À La recherche du temps perdu* deals with themes of time, memory, art and finances, as well as exploring the position of the author/narrator.

A nostalgic note for times past (pp. 110–11) is replaced by the recollection of the trip to America with its excitement and glamour (p. 112). The detail of the earth from Stratford-upon-Avon in the urn carries associations with the Dracula legend; at times, elsewhere, Melchior is seen as this menacing, Dracula-like creature. Peregrine too has similar elements of menace beneath the jovial exterior; Carter portrays the main male characters as powerful, dominant and threatening, yet exuding that fascinating charisma which frequently accompanies these qualities. A brief glimpse of pathos emerges in Peregrine's morning out in New York with Dora to the site of the old Plaza theatre, the place where his parents met their untimely end. Peregrine chooses to take Dora on this 'pilgrimage', not Nora, because while 'He loved us both', Dora confides, 'I was the one he talked to' (p. 116).

The extravagant glamour of the apartment that Peregrine seems to be sharing with Delia Delaney/Daisy Duck is matched by Daisy's outrageous behaviour and comments on first meeting the twins. On seeing the two young girls in the flat, Daisy's first words are 'When does the orgy begin?' (p. 115); her first action is to throw a phone out of the fifteenth-floor window. Her past encapsulates the rise to fame of many Hollywood stars. The humble origins, her childhood appearances, the nickname, the screen image and the style – 'She'd got real style, she could put on a show' (p. 116) – suggest several stars of the period.

The journey across America (pp. 116–20) and the first impressions of Hollywood (pp. 120–4) have **carnivalesque** qualities throughout. The story is typically interspersed with brief, characteristic portrayals of Daisy with her public and private images; Peregrine with his size and his magic; Nora with yet another affair; and Dora herself with her less impetuous involvement with men, in this case the hard-drinking, literate Irish. His role as part-time lover and educator – 'he gave me Culture' (p. 123) – accounts for the literary erudition that complements Dora's colloquial style (although, as she admits, 'I balked at Proust').

GLOSSARY

112	**Schiaparelli** (1890–1973) Italian-born French fashion designer
113	**El Greco** Spanish name meaning 'the Greek', nickname of artist Domenikos Theotocopoulos (1541–1614)
114	*embarras de richesse* abundance of options
115	**Prohibition** period from 1920 to 1933 when the manufacture and sale of alcohol were banned in the USA
120	**Chekhov** Anton Chekhov (1860–1904), Russian dramatist and short-story writer
	Anne Hathaway's cottage home of Shakespeare's wife in Stratford-upon-Avon, still a tourist attraction today

PAGES 124–40

- The set and the cast of *A Midsummer Night's Dream* are described.
- Daisy Duck turns out to be the wife of the producer, Genghis Khan.
- The first day on the set and Melchior's speech are described.
- There is a résumé of the character and the past of Genghis Khan.

CHECK THE BOOK

'A knowledge of Shakespeare's *A Midsummer Night's Dream* will help you appreciate the similarities and differences as well as the **allusions** in *Wise Children*. A good edition with an extensive introduction and detailed explanatory notes is the Arden Shakespeare, edited by Harold F. Brooks.

The set of the wood near Athens for *A Midsummer Night's Dream* is an extravagantly literal interpretation of the text of the play with added Hollywood technological innovations. Even tiny wild animals are ready for scattering across the set. Dora recalls the significance of the event in the light of the Notting Hill cinema visit (pp. 110–11). She reflects on the transience of stardom and the permanence of film. There are amusing descriptions of the dwarfs hired by Genghis Khan, the film producer.

King Oberon is to be played by Melchior; and Titania, his queen, by Daisy Duck. It turns out that she is the wife of Genghis Khan. Dora catalogues Daisy's positive qualities, but sums her up rather bluntly: 'But class – no' (p. 127).

During the pre-production exercises Melchior telephones, and Dora's reaction to his voice is once again romantic. Melchior is now ensconced as the leader of the English set in Hollywood, and his call is to remind the girls that he needs the urn of Stratford earth for the opening ceremony. It has been misplaced, but is eventually found in a closet, flanked by candles and incense: the Catholic Mexican cleaning lady had treated it as a holy relic. Unfortunately Daisy's cat had used it as a litter tray, so the earth is tipped out of the window and replaced by earth from the hotel garden – rather aptly and **ironically** called the Forest of Arden.

> **CONTEXT**
> The forest of Arden, a wooded area of Warwickshire, is the setting for *As You Like It*.

The opening ceremony is vivid in Dora's memory, and she soon realises that the film is destined to be a financial disaster. People are described in brief, typical snapshots – the acrobatic and oversexed Puck; Irish, drunk and supported by his friend Peregrine; the image-conscious Daisy Duck; and the dominant producer complete with jodhpurs, whip and the canvas chair. One odd figure, a small woman in raincoat, dark glasses and headscarf, stands out. She seems to be following Daisy.

Melchior makes his grand entrance to music, bearing the urn on a cushion. His first words are cut short by Genghis Khan, who is appalled by Melchior's revealing tights. Melchior is furious, but realises that his mission to take Shakespeare to America could be at stake. Peregrine saves the day by producing magically a macaw from the bulge in Melchior's tights, thereby ending the 'Mexican standoff' (p. 133).

> **CONTEXT**
> A Mexican standoff is a saying which suggests a situation in which no resolution can be expected, where no side can emerge a winner.

In his overinflated speech, Melchior acknowledges Nora and Dora as the bearers of the casket but he refers to them as his nieces. Dora spots the attraction between Daisy and Melchior, which is apparent in their eyes and in his tights.

Genghis Khan's power over aspiring young actresses is clear; the photograph of his wife Daisy in his office shows them the possibilities; his casting couch is the possible means. Daisy's feeding of a live carp to her Persian cat matches her husband's ruthlessness. The mysterious lady on the set is revealed as the producer's first wife from Brooklyn, who has been stalking Daisy.

While Genghis believes that his money will keep Daisy in check, she proves him wrong when she and Melchior make love on the set during a lunch break.

COMMENTARY

Hollywood now adds its own ethos to the carnivalesque elements. In the 'Land of Make-Believe' we are greeted with 'Welcome to Dreamland' (p. 120). However, the dreams are of a different nature. Dora, in fact, tells us that there was no illusion. The hotel is patently artificial; the film set is 'too solid' and 'too literal' in its interpretation of Shakespeare's play and the wood near Athens (p. 125). The set is 'custom-made' and there is a proliferation of detail in the artificiality and complexity of the set, the cast, the costumes and the props.

Dora's reflection on the making of the film and films in general is not fully realised until much later in time. The visit to the squalid cinema in Notting Hill (pp. 110–11) contrasts with the illusory glamour of Hollywood. Furthermore, Dora's thoughts in Hollywood contrast with her thoughts years later after the recognition of the young man who seeks her autograph.

Initial roles and changing roles in the film are appropriate in the context of Hollywood and in real life. Melchior is King Oberon; his queen (with limited lines to speak) is Daisy Duck, soon to be his second wife. Puck is played by an undersized, oversexed tiny man. Nora and Dora are, quite naturally, singing and dancing fairies, while there are even extra roles for Saskia and Imogen, created by Peregrine, who has co-written the script with Irish and, as an afterthought, William Shakespeare.

Irish's affair with Dora serves two purposes, besides presenting a colourful, possibly archetypal character – the wild, rambunctious, hard-drinking, literate but disillusioned writer. He educates Dora, thereby accounting for the literary qualities of her writing and the many references and **allusions** to other works of fiction that scatter the text. Dora also lets him have his say with a cruel character portrayal of her in his 'famous *Hollywood* stories' (p. 119). We question whether this portrait of Dora – 'the treacherous, lecherous

CHECK THE FILM

It might be useful to compare different cinematic portrayals of the character Puck – he was played by Mickey Rooney in the 1935 film, and by Stanley Tucci in the 1999 version.

chorus girl' – is accurate, recognisable or exaggerated, and it is Carter's way of telling us to make our own minds up about the narrator and also about Irish himself.

Melchior is king both on the film set and with the 'English Colony' (p. 127) in Hollywood. His role is dealt with at greater length in **Characterisation**, but there are a number of features worth noting here. His role as an ambassador of the British Empire and the missionary bringer of culture to the colonies calls to mind Ranulph, his father. Carter's exploration of the theme of a declining empire is expanded in her portrayal of inconsequentialities and the aloofness of the English Colony. The failure of the film, along with Melchior's attempts to recapture America (expressed almost literally), is foreshadowed in the carnivalesque opening ceremony (pp. 129–37). The symbolism of the urn with its sacred Stratford-upon-Avon earth is turned on its head as the cat-soiled earth is replaced by soil from a different Forest of Arden, the hotel grounds. Oblivious to the switch, Melchior grandly holds the urn aloft 'as if it were the Holy Grail' (p. 114). His speech is a **pastiche**, a **parody** of theatrical oratory. The **farcical** incident arising from the bulge in his tights causes Genghis to rant and rage, but Peregrine is able to use the carnivalesque spirit of magic to defuse the situation by producing a macaw from Melchior's crotch.

Dora's ability here as narrator and observer is at its best. She tells us she is 'little Miss Sharp Eyes' (p. 137) and her eye roves everywhere, so that we have a panoramic panning across the scene and zoom-in focus on the many people present. The cataloguing and unfolding of the main events are interspersed with glimpses of, variously, Peregrine, Irish, Puck, Daisy Duck, Genghis and others in typical activity. Dora's ability to reduce the intended sublime to the ridiculous is seen in details such as the macaw dropping a message from above 'with a lingering SPLAT!' (p. 135) or Irish being sick (p. 136). The language frequently descends to the low. Puck 'copped hold' of Dora's hand (p. 136); Dora's comment about tuning lutes is both out of place and appropriate at the same time (p. 129); and there is even an ambiguity about Melchior's two-fingered 'benediction' (p. 137).

CONTEXT

The Holy Grail was the cup supposedly used by Christ at the Last Supper and in which Joseph of Arimathea received Christ's blood; the quest for it is the source of many medieval legends, particularly the Arthurian tales.

The portrait of Genghis Khan is a parody of the archetypal Hollywood film mogul. It develops through costume and props, his casting-couch proclivities, his ultra-chauvinistic predatory attitude to women, his belligerent voice and his dictatorial rule over his kingdom the size of Monaco. The excesses of his wedding night with Daisy sum up the decadence, perhaps the whole spirit, of the place.

CHECK THE BOOK

The portrayals of Genghis Khan and Daisy Duck are in many ways parodies of figures in the Hollywood film industry. Kate Webb in her essay 'Seriously Funny: *Wise Children*', suggests possible parallels in real life (see p. 296 of *Flesh and the Mirror: Essays on the Art of Angela Carter* edited by Lorna Sage).

GLOSSARY		
124	*faux*	false
126	**Brown Derby**	Hollywood restaurant
127	**chutzpah**	impudence, shameless, boldness
128	**hoi polloi**	the common people, the masses
129	**yarmulke**	a skullcap worn by Jewish males
130	**Schopenhauer**	(1788–1860) German philosopher
131	**B-feature**	low-budget film used to support the main feature
	Stokowski	(1882–1977) American conductor and occasional film actor
	galliard	a lively dance popular in the sixteenth and seventeenth centuries
136	**mechanical**	the tradesmen of Athens are referred to by this term in *A Midsummer Night's Dream*

PAGES 140–52

- In Hollywood the girls enter the routine of dance rehearsals.
- Dora's affair with Irish ends.
- Peregrine leaves to buy a ranch in Texas.
- Daisy Duck reveals that she is pregnant and confronts Melchior as the father.
- Divorces are arranged and triple engagements are announced.
- The filming finally comes to an end.

Dora describes the routine of rehearsals and dance practice. The affair between Melchior and Daisy is clear to all, including Lady Atalanta. Peregrine's fondness for his daughters, Saskia and Imogen, is described, though Melchior, their 'father', comes first in their eyes. There are further excesses in the film's interpretation of the play.

Dora's affair with Irish comes to an end. Nora's relationship with the Italian boy, however, continues.

Dora feels they are 'victims of a plot', 'marooned in Wonderland' (p. 142), and ascribes this to the finances that drive the film industry. She longs for home and Grandma Chance, particularly when Nora reveals her desire to 'take instruction' and marry Tony (p. 149). Suddenly Perry leaves for Hazard, Texas, the place where Ranulph and Estella had played years ago.

Daisy announces that she is pregnant, and refuses to pass the child off as Genghis's. Nora suggests that the producer really wants children, having learnt this from Genghis himself, when he tells her bluntly that he has chosen her to be the mother of his child. Nora's refusal causes Genghis to admit a desire for revenge on Melchior, whom Daisy is determined to marry. Desperate, Genghis then suggests that Dora might consider bearing him a child.

Daisy gatecrashes a game of cricket at the Hazard home to reveal the news of her pregnancy to Melchior. Lady Atalanta, maintaining her dignity, allows Daisy to take Melchior, and a 'swift Mexican divorce' ensues (p. 148). By now, Dora believes that the film is heading towards disaster.

Nora persuades Dora to answer the phone to Genghis Khan and accept his offer of marriage. Three engagements are announced – Daisy to Melchior, Nora to Tony and Dora to Genghis. The girls send telegrams with news of the engagements to Grandma Chance. Dora and Genghis become the centre of media attention, and Dora inherits the nuisance calls from his first wife. There is still no news from Grandma Chance, nor any word from Peregrine.

Gorgeous George appears on the set to play Bottom. Unfortunately George's humour does not transfer to America and his part is cut to a minimum.

CONTEXT

To 'take instruction' here means to be educated in the teachings of the Roman Catholic faith.

CHECK THE FILM

Renowned Shakespearian director Sir Peter Hall made a film of *A Midsummer Night's Dream* in 1969, based on his earlier Royal Shakespeare Company stage production. The impressive cast includes Judi Dench as Titania, Ian Richardson as Oberon and Ian Holm as Puck. The costumes, which include miniskirts, capture the feel of 'swinging' London in the late 1960s.

COMMENTARY

The 'dreary time', the 'sweated labour' and the 'love of Mammon' present a bleak picture of the reality behind the glamour of Hollywood (p. 140 and p. 143). Dora's portrayal of this underside of the film industry dominates this section. Peregrine's disappearance, described in a typically abrupt manner, further outlandish interpretations of the play and a sense that the film will fail financially add to the sinking feeling.

Daisy's announcement that she is pregnant reveals a peculiar honesty about paternity that reflects on the central issue in Dora's mind. It also leads to a splendid **farcical** scene in front of Melchior and the English Colony which demonstrates the cinematographic qualities of Carter's writing, with its images, dialogue, suggested sound effects and perfect timing.

Dora's aside on Melchior's ambitions – 'I think he thought that he was marrying … Hollywood itself, taking over the entire factory' (p. 148) – places him in a broader perspective and is worth looking at in the light of the later discoveries in the bedroom in his London home (Chapter 5, pp. 224–5).

The sudden reappearance of Gorgeous George (last seen on Brighton Pier) is Peregrine's final act of manipulation before his disappearance. Is he aware that the comedy that George offers will not travel well? Is he using this to undermine Melchior's success? Neither question, like many in the novel, can be definitively answered, but they are worth posing in the light of other incidents between the two brothers. George's failure in America suggests the decline of the music hall in the face of the growth of cinema at this time. Dora comments that 'Gorgeous George's stab at global fame was dying on its feet' (p. 151). In a more symbolic sense, given his patriotic performances of the past, his dated plus fours and the map of the world on his body, Carter may be adding to the debate about the decline of the British Empire.

 CHECK THE BOOK

On p. 287 of her essay 'Seriously Funny: *Wise Children*', Kate Webb places Melchior and the English Colony in a broader perspective thematically (in *Flesh and the Mirror: Essays on the Art of Angela Carter*, edited by Lorna Sage).

GLOSSARY

143	**panhandle** narrow strip of land between one state and another
144	*hors de combat* out of the fight
	lox smoked salmon
	Wedekind Frank Wedekind (1864–1918), German dramatist
145	**Grünewald** early fifteenth-century German painter in the Gothic style
146	**Cooper's Oxford** noted Oxford-based producer of traditional marmalade
147	**Arpège** perfume produced by the Lanvin house
149	**Hedda Hopper ... Louella Parsons** rival film gossip columnists
	ecru greyish-yellow colour
	Photoplay popular film magazine

PAGES 152–62

- The end of filming is accompanied by a triple engagement party.
- Dora meets the first wife of Genghis Khan, who takes Dora's place in the subsequent wedding ceremony.
- Peregrine enters on a white horse to conduct the wedding ceremonies.
- Grandma Chance arrives and takes Dora and Nora home with her.
- It turns out that Daisy is not pregnant after all.

QUESTION
This is one of Peregrine's many dramatic appearances. They, along with his disappearances, have a legendary, mysterious and at times magical quality. What does this suggest about the romantic view of his life?

As filming comes to an end, the celebrations begin. The entire cast and staff are present, although Lady Atalanta has stayed away. Irish, drunk as usual, presents Dora with the proofs of his book, dedicated to her, his 'gilded fly' (p. 152). Genghis gives Dora a massive engagement ring, but he still gazes helplessly at Daisy clinging to Melchior 'like skin round sausage' (p. 153).

Dora muses on sadness and tragedy, putting things into perspective. Escaping to the bathroom, she feels that she has sold herself. Wandering onto the set, she is shocked to see her double. It is not Nora, but the first wife of Genghis, who has transformed herself into a replica of Dora. Hearing the Wedding March, Dora panics and switches places with the ex-wife, hastily giving her the engagement ring 'as if it were a burning coal' (p. 156).

Now in need of a disguise herself, Dora stumbles over the unconscious George. Stealing his costume, she goes to her own wedding dressed as Bottom.

In the confusion at the party, Tony's mamma appears. While she is berating her son, a cowboy on a huge white horse enters to cheers and applause; as soon as he speaks, Dora recognises Peregrine. As sheriff of Hazard, Texas, he performs the wedding ceremony. However, as the three rings are placed on the three fingers, Tony's mamma tips marinara sauce all over Nora, and champagne corks popping are mistaken for gunfire.

In the chaos, Dora, still in the Bottom costume, makes her way outdoors. There she bumps into Grandma Chance, who has pawned the grandfather clock to finance the flight out. The girls and Daisy's white cat return to England. Tony's mamma gets her way and his marriage to Nora is over. It emerges that Daisy is not pregnant, a revelation which swiftly brings about the end of her marriage to Melchior. He returns to London, his Hollywood dream over. The war, 'declared in the nick of time' (p. 161), turns him into a hero. Daisy, admired by Dora for her 'go' (p. 162), survives by acting in American soaps.

COMMENTARY

The **carnivalesque** celebrations demonstrate once more the filmic qualities of the text, creating a wildly comic scene of gargantuan proportions. It involves disguises, mistaken identities, unexpected entrances, chaotic scenes, parallels with Shakespeare's play and farcical, pantomimic comedy.

Dora's recollections – 'I always misremember' (p. 157) – place the events in the broader context of credibility, but do not detract

> **CONTEXT**
>
> By drawing on all our senses, Carter enables her readers to enjoy the full **farcical** effect of this chaotic wedding scene.

from our enjoyment or willing suspension of disbelief in the carnivalesque denouement.

The events, as elsewhere, are heralded by a 'brisk wind' (p. 157), this time not from the Hollywood wind machine. The sense that something is about to happen needs no direct statement for a reader attuned to the way things operate. Suddenly the illusory world is transformed and the enchanted forest becomes a menacing presence, a wood of fairy tale become real. Repetition of 'wood' builds up the menace: it becomes 'the wood that changes you; the wood where you go mad; the wood where the shadows live longer than you do' (p. 155).

 CHECK THE FILM

In 2005 the BBC adapted four Shakespeare plays into modern English. *A Midsummer Night's Dream* was set in the Dream Park holiday resort over a luxury weekend, with entertainment supplied by the Rude Mechanicals. The series, *Shakespeare Retold*, is now available on video and DVD.

This dark, brooding moment contrasts with the hilarity which follows. It begins with an excessive series of entertainments, put on by Genghis, which are catalogued to absurdity (pp. 152–3). There are the expected cameo pictures from Dora's roving observant eye as she picks out familiar faces in the crowd. The catalogue technique itself is **parodied** at the end of what we might expect to be a large crowd of 'fairies, goblins, spirits, mice, rabbits, badgers' with the open-ended 'etc. etc. etc.' (p. 158), which leaves the reader to imagine the rest and take part in the absurd excesses of Genghis's production. Events mirror in a distorted fashion parts of the plot of *A Midsummer Night's Dream* with lovers lost and found, disguises, false identities, revelations, marriages and the worlds of illusion and reality. The theme of doubling now reaches its climax with Genghis's first wife mistaken for Dora in a successful yet absurdly comic imitation (she has had so much plastic surgery in an attempt to look like Dora that 'Her face was lifted up so far her ears had ended up on top of her head'). Dora, meanwhile, has taken on the disguise of Bottom, complete with the ass's head and plus fours of Gorgeous George. Shakespeare, music hall and narrator are neatly rolled into one. George, along with his map, has been pushed aside and hidden from sight literally and metaphorically.

Peregrine reaches new heights of **melodramatic** magic in his entrance on a white horse. Lutenists absurdly attempting to play 'Home on the Range', the 'clip-clop' of the horse resembling sound effects on stage, the sight of the 'biggest cowpoke' and finally the voice all prepare the reader for the revelation by Dora that this is Peregrine. The realisation of the rest of the crowd is kept for the next stage in the unfolding farce, as the popping of champagne corks is mistaken for gunfire. Thus, with the crowd lying flat on the ground, the horse rears and Perry is vividly revealed.

The chaos that ensues enables Carter to resolve the problems of three marriages, two of which are swiftly annulled. Musing on the third, Dora tells us that 'Genghis Khan and the imitation Dora lived happily ever after … and if you believe that, you'll believe anything' (p. 161). The dramatic entrance of Grandma Chance is heralded by a familiar odour, the ass recognising Grandma but she profanely failing to penetrate Dora's disguise, so that, as with Peregrine, we anticipate her arrival. Her return to England with the girls and Daisy's cat seems almost inevitable.

This final section is a fine example of Carter's eclectic style, which combines several elements. In the unfolding of the novel we have surreal images and perspectives (Dora in a double 'I' identity watching her own marriage and crying inside an ass's head); Shakespearian references (the 'beast with two backs' is from *Othello*); mirrors of the past (Hazard in Texas is the place where Ranulph wore his cardboard crown); gossipy asides (the **allusion** to the 'silver-fox trenches' and where they came from); a parody of **narrative** style ('There I go again! Can't keep a story going in a straight line, can I? Drunk in charge of a narrative'); a return to the reality of war, which here has a touch of the absurd, as it is 'declared in the nick of time', and a touch of theatre as Melchior is 'turned into a war hero', almost like another role; and the faded ending of the chapter in Dora's **voice** ('Still on the go. I was always fond of Daisy').

CHECK THE BOOK

Gina Wisker suggests that 'Art, design and the nature of reality are all brought to mind when a play based on a dream is transferred to the Dream Factory' (*Angela Carter: A Beginner's Guide*, 2003).

GLOSSARY

152	**The Boar's Head in Hand Bear I** a carol which traditionally accompanies the carrying in of a cooked boar to a feast, particularly at Christmas, when it was customary for boar to be served
153	**Bryn Mawr** college in Pennsylvania
	Algonquin large, luxurious New York hotel
154	**Pulitzer** annual prizes, first awarded in 1917, for achievements in literature, film, music and journalism

CHAPTER 4

PAGES 163–78

- Dora selectively recalls the war years and its effects on the family.
- The girls are now in their thirties and tour in pantomime and music hall.
- They keep in touch with Lady Atalanta.
- Peregrine returns and they attend the twenty-first birthday party of Saskia and Imogen.
- Melchior announces his marriage to one of Saskia's friends, and the party ends in disorder.
- Peregrine leaves for South America.

Dora dismisses the war from her **memoirs**, though she does recall odd, inconsequential memories. There is no news of Peregrine on secret service duties. Nora and Dora feel that Grandma's death is the end of childhood; with her death goes the twins' only witness of their birth.

The girls are now in their thirties. Their tiresome touring in shows, pantomimes and finally the nude revues traces the decline of theatre in the forties and fifties. However, high culture, with Melchior in Shakespearian roles, is popular.

Nora and Dora start to visit Lady Atalanta at Lynde Court Home Farm. Lady Atalanta lives a simple life, attended by Old Nanny. She receives nothing from Melchior, though he lavishes presents on the girls; and her bedroom is a shrine to her ex-husband.

Lady Atalanta invites Dora and Nora to the twenty-first birthday celebrations for Imogen and Saskia. As they debate about whether to attend, there is an unexpected call from Peregrine, who offers to drive them down.

CONTEXT

Saskia, playing Perdita in *The Winter's Tale*, quotes from the play in a barbed reference to Dora and Nora's illegitimacy (p. 166). The name Perdita means 'lost one'; in *The Winter's Tale* she is abandoned by her father, who believes her to be illegitimate. In the light of what we learn about Saskia and Imogen's parentage, however, the **allusion** is doubly pertinent.

Peregrine has changed little, except he seems to be 'bigger than ever' (p. 170). His fortunes are high from an oil find on his Texas ranch, yet beneath his joviality he seems on edge. Saskia is doing the cooking for the party. Her best friend has been chosen to play Cordelia to Melchior's King Lear.

A strange outdoor meal ensues. Peregrine presents Saskia and Imogen with a rare caterpillar each, named after the two girls. Imogen shows her disappointment, Saskia sarcastic disapproval; and Peregrine is upset. Melchior announces his present – a new stepmother. He intends to marry his Cordelia, Saskia's best friend. Dora recalls the earlier Hazard marriage of a Lear and a Cordelia and the subsequent tragedy. In the ensuing chaos and tantrums, the caterpillars are squashed.

Peregrine announces his decision to return to South America. Nora remarks that he and Grandma Chance should have made a go of it.

COMMENTARY

The reality of war is dismissed by Dora: 'it was no carnival' (p. 163). As such, Dora does not want it to intrude on her story. The oddity and inconsequentiality of memories are realistic in their own way. The cock crowing in Bond Street, the surreal image of a zebra galloping down Camden High Street, flowers on the bomb sites and the 'patriotic pig' serve to illustrate the way memory can be selective and can put horrors in perspective (p. 163). The emergence of the realities of war almost as passing references in the **narrative** (Grandma's death, the Blitz, the loss of Cyn's husband in North Africa) does not negate their significance in Dora's life. 'I have my memories,' she tells us firmly, 'but I prefer to keep them to myself, thank you very much' (p. 163).

Peregrine's mysterious action off stage, as it were, is continued in his work in the secret service and his ability in a time of austerity to lay his hands on a case of crème de menthe and a barrel of Guinness for the funeral party (p. 164).

There is a poignant passage which places Grandma's death into the broader context of life and its realities beyond the carnival.

> **CONTEXT**
>
> Again and again Shakespeare appears, indelibly woven into the fabric of Dora's story. The quote on p. 163 – the 'funeral baked meats' – comes from *Hamlet* (I.2.180).

CHECK THE BOOK

Angela Carter talks about carnival in an interview with Lorna Sage in *New Writing* (edited by Malcolm Bradbury and Judith Cooke, 1992).

The silence of the house, the tears, the recollection that they have lost the only witness to their birth and their childhood, the image of their mother as 'that ghost without a face' (p. 164) and the guilt at their mockery of Grandma Chance's nakedness in old age provide numerous images that contrast with the **carnivalesque** dominance in the story. Further details of the austerity of life in post-war Britain appear throughout this phase of the story. The growing gap between high and low culture, the last gasp of the music halls and the desperate last attempts at survival in the nude revues complete a bleak picture.

Saskia and Imogen's twenty-first birthday party brings together the Hazard family, legitimate and illegitimate. A darkly comic scene unfolds, sinisterly carnivalesque in several of its elements. In the original spirit of medieval carnival, excesses were not confined to pleasures, but did have elements of violence. The scene, and what takes place afterwards, displays some of the unpleasant aspects of individuals, notably Saskia and her evil culinary intentions, Melchior with his self-centred announcement, and Saskia and Imogen with their mercenary outlook and their rejection of not just Peregrine's gifts but of both parents.

GLOSSARY	
165	**a.s.m.** assistant stage manager
	Oliver Messel set and costume designer in the 1930s and 1940s
167	**Sarah Bernhardt** (1844–1927) French actress who made several visits to the USA
	The Duse Eleonora Duse (1859–1924), Italian actress, rival of Bernhardt
	Ellen Terry (1847–1928) British Shakespearian actress
	Mrs Miniver film set in England during the Second World War
169	**VJ Day** day marking Japan's surrender to the Allies: 15 August 1945
171	**Caesar's wife** Calpurnia, who remained faithful in spite of Julius Caesar's infidelities and neglect

PAGES 178–93

- Dora recounts the events following the disintegration of Saskia and Imogen's twenty-first birthday party.
- Now confined to a wheelchair and destitute, Lady Atalanta is taken in by Nora and Dora.
- Saskia finds success as a television cook. Later she seduces the young Tristram as revenge on her family.
- Tristram's involvement with Tiffany is compromised by his affair with Saskia.
- In the present, Nora, Dora and Wheelchair dress for Melchior's one hundredth birthday party.

Back in Bard Road following Saskia and Imogen's twenty-first birthday party, Nora and Dora are filled in by Old Nanny on events following the birthday party. Lady Atalanta has fallen down the stairs and is wheelchair bound. It is never made clear whether she fell, or was pushed. Saskia and Imogen have left, and have made their mother sign over Home Farm and her last bit of capital to them. Dora and Nora take in Lady Atalanta.

> **CONTEXT**
> Dora and Nora live, appropriately, at 49 Bard Road in London. From the late nineteenth century Shakespeare was known as the Bard of Avon.

Saskia prospers as a television cook. When Tristram, one of Melchior's sons by his third wife, is still at school, Saskia writes to him, and on a half-term visit she seduces him. Dora believes this to be part of her revenge on the Hazard family.

Dora muses on Peregrine's visits to Gunter Grove and Tristram's similarities to him. Nora and Dora believe that he is the father of the twins Tristram and Gareth, though Gareth's similarities to Melchior leave the matter open to speculation. Tristram continues the affair with Saskia, though he has several girlfriends, including Tiffany.

Lady Atalanta's daughters have remained indifferent to her for forty years. Back in the present, Nora and Dora resolve that Wheelchair will accompany them to Melchior's one hundredth birthday party. Dora suggests they swap their traditional perfumes, as they had done long ago.

Dora and Nora search through all the clothes they have stored in Grandma Chance's bedroom. The photographs on the mantelpiece chart the girls' past with Grandma and Peregrine, whom they now believe to be dead. The search through the old clothes evokes memories of the past. They reminisce about their illegitimacy and muse on their present old age without children. The spirit of Grandma also makes a haphazardly supernatural appearance in the tumbling of her garments from the wardrobe.

A trip to Brixton market produces shiny stockings, short skirts, gold stilettos, cheap beads and earrings. They take pains over their make-up. They enjoy the transformation, but admit cheerfully to the effect: 'painted harlots, and over the hill' (p. 192). Wheelchair still remains faithful to the memory of Melchior. The April showers remind them of the date, the twenty-third of April, the birthday shared by the girls, Melchior, Peregrine and William Shakespeare. Dora reflects on Melchior's destiny to play Shakespeare and their fate to sing and dance.

> **CONTEXT**
>
> William Shakespeare's actual date of birth is not known for certain, but his birthday is traditionally celebrated on 23 April – St George's Day. He was baptised in Holy Trinity Church, Stratford-upon-Avon, on Wednesday 26 April 1564, and no more than a few days are likely to have elapsed between his birth and his baptism. He died on 23 April 1616.

COMMENTARY

The phone call from Old Nanny provides the **narrative** shift necessary to reconstruct events after the departure of Dora and Nora from Lynde Court Home Farm.

The dualities and distorted mirror **motifs** are given a further dimension here in the mercenary, selfish Saskia and Imogen and the altruistic, charitable Dora and Nora. Old Nanny's retention in the Hazard family enables her to report on other events and speculations in another **voice**.

A **parody** of celebrity television cookery programmes depicts Saskia cutting up a hare: 'voluptuous' is one adjective that sets the tone for her performance, and it is worth noting the development of this aspect (pp. 180–1). The movement from the television studio to the bedroom is neatly described in the balance of 'She jugged a hare for Tristram, once, that cooked his goose' (p. 181). Saskia's seduction of Tristram is a reversal of the male incestuous seductions in the Hazard family. Dora's despising of Saskia is put into perspective in the slightly admiring alliteration of 'Saskia, the sexy sexuagenarian' and in her half-admission of jealousy (p. 184).

Nora's sudden question 'What shall we wear tonight?' punctuates the story and returns us to the present as evening approaches. However, no sooner are we back in the present before another digression takes us to Tuscany, to Saskia's villa, where Saskia seems to have doctored the food again to take Tiffany out of the way so that she can lay her hands on Tristram.

The preparations for the party permit nostalgic links with past events that have already been narrated by Dora. The exploration of Grandma Chance's bedroom with its many photographs and wardrobe full of clothes takes us back through time and place, even to the navy blue bloomers of the dancing class. Nora calls the collection 'A history of the world in party frocks' (p. 187). Memories of past lovers (pp. 188–9) eventually lead to a musing by Dora on time and old age, but an eerie moment halts the nostalgia. The flickering light and the propulsion of Grandma Chance's little toque across the room, followed by an avalanche of gloves 'whirling around as if inhabited by hands' and the creaking of the wardrobe door, all seem to Dora and Nora to be the voice of Grandma speaking to them in a familiar tone with a familiar message to close the door to the past and 'Expect the worst, hope for the best!' (p. 190).

This cameo scene throws the story firmly back into present time and the final preparations for the party. We are prepared for the carnival spirit that characterises the climax of the novel. The deliberate introduction of the word 'hags' calls to mind Bakhtin's depiction of the old woman who reminds us of the life cycle and the regenerative power of carnival. Nora and Dora in garish costume that even they admit is over the top become the spirit that recalls at once birth, life, death and change. Their transformation into the 'painted harlots' (p. 192) that they were accused of being years ago has echoes of that earlier transformation of the two into the Lucky Chances. Carter is reminding us that the female image in a male-orientated world is a construct.

The sympathetic background of rain at the window, April showers, recalls those earlier birthdays that 'doomed' Melchior to wear his pasteboard crown and Nora and Dora to sing and dance (p. 193).

 CHECK THE NET
S. L. Deefholts summarises Bakhtin's description of the carnival's image of the laughing hag who is heavily pregnant in Part 3 of 'Hazarding Chance: Reading Angela Carter's *Wise Children*'. To read this essay, go to **www.angelfire.com** and follow the links to 'Arts' and 'Online Writing' and search for the author's name.

Allusions to Shakespeare and Charlie Chaplin complete the reminder of the legitimate and non-legitimate worlds that different branches of the Hazard/Chance family inhabit.

GLOSSARY	
179	**teddibly** phonetic spelling of 'terribly' in an exaggerated British upper-class accent
181	*Harper's Bazaar* American fashion magazine
	crème renversée type of French custard dessert
	Cascara evacuant a laxative preparation
185	*trippa fiorentina* tripe in a tomato sauce from Florence, Italy
191	**Old Bill** William Shakespeare
192	**Miss Haversham** in Dickens's *Great Expectations* (1860–1) Miss Havisham, jilted on her wedding day, has worn her bridal gown ever since

CHAPTER 5

PAGES 194–206

- Dora, Nora and Wheelchair attend the one hundredth birthday celebrations for Sir Melchior.
- Dora recognises Gorgeous George begging in the street.
- There is some acknowledgement of fatherhood from Melchior.
- Daisy Duck appears in flamboyant style.
- Tristram arrives, looking drawn and ill.
- Just as the cake is about to be cut, there is a tremendous knocking at the door.

CONTEXT

The opening two paragraphs of the final chapter recall the opening paragraphs of Chapter 1, both in style and content.

The girls cross the river and approach the Hazard residence. It is surrounded by media. An attendant carries Wheelchair in his arms up the stairs. For a moment her eyes flash and she seems to be the beautiful Lady Atalanta of long ago.

Dora recognises Gorgeous George, who is begging in the street. She gives him a twenty-pound note. He fails to recognise her, though her references to *The Dream* produce an odd look from him. Dora's Shakespearian farewell is for him to go and 'drink a health to bastards' (p. 197). Dora and Nora march up the steps to the party; at the top of the staircase they glimpse each other in the mirror and are shocked and amused, but ultimately defiant.

Dora is struck by the extravagant luxury of the decor. The smell of lilac recalls the past. Melchior is seated on a throne-like chair receiving a line of guests. The girls join the queue and Dora recalls the first meeting with her father years ago. The third Lady Hazard is scanning the room, clearly looking for Tristram. Melchior greets the girls as Peaseblossom and Mustardseed, their roles in *The Dream*. Both Nora and Dora call him 'Dad' and he hugs them (p. 200). They are weeping, but enjoy this moment of recognition and love.

Nora nibbles a chicken thigh until she recognises from the rosemary recipe that Saskia is doing the catering. They find Wheelchair in the toilet with Old Nanny. She still feels guilty that she betrayed Melchior with Peregrine. They wheel her into the ballroom, where she is hidden behind a statue.

To a fanfare of trumpets Daisy Duck makes her entrance. She is drunk but her glamour still commands attention; and she and Melchior make up their past differences. She is accompanied by a tiny man. Daisy recognises the girls and then Lady Atalanta with delight.

Tristram now enters. He looks ill and is supported by his aunts, Imogen and Saskia. Wheelchair is clearly distressed at seeing her daughters. Saskia is dressed fashionably; Imogen is wearing a fishbowl on her head, complete with a live fish, a walking commercial for her *Goldie the Goldfish* children's show. Dora recalls Tristram's treatment of Tiffany and has no sympathy for him. At a signal from Saskia the cake is brought in. Saskia hands Melchior a sword. As he prepares to cut the cake, there is a tremendous knocking at the door.

> **CONTEXT**
>
> At his party Melchior wears 'a rather majestic and heavily embroidered purple caftan', prompting Dora to think, somewhat maliciously, 'colostomy' (p. 198). A colostomy is a surgical operation to remove a damaged part of the colon; the cut end is diverted to an opening in the stomach and a bag is attached to collect waste products from the body.

COMMENTARY

The **carnivalesque** atmosphere reaches its climax in the final chapter. Ahead of the glamour of the Hazard family gathering there are small asides worth noting: the 'other side' reminder, the sword simile with its various possible interpretations, the patriarchal reference to 'Old *Father* Thames', and the vague sense of menace in the bushes which 'crouched like bears' and the 'pale and ghostly' tulips (p. 194).

Reality is firmly established in the media clamour outside the Hazard residence. The beggar tugging at Dora's sleeve belongs to this real world, but he first causes Dora to reflect on the selectivity and idiosyncrasy of memory with three personal examples (p. 195). Half forgotten, rather like a ghost at the feast, Gorgeous George makes his final shabby appearance. He causes Dora to reflect on 'untimely death' (p. 196), but it is the faded pink of his continents beneath the faded ex-army greatcoat that thematically portrays the decline of empire.

Shakespearian references emerge once more, both indirect (such as his face on the twenty-pound note) and direct (for example Dora's recollection of George as Bottom in *The Dream* and her free quotation in her farewell to him).

The mirror at the top of the stairs throws back a **parody** of their former selves, but, able to laugh at their 'overdone' appearance, this does not deter them from seizing the day and, in modern parlance, 'strutting their stuff' (p. 198). The setting, too, is overdone, recalling perhaps the 'too august a setting' of Lynde Court (Chapter 2, p. 96). One detail in the catalogue of extravagance, the glasses 'reflected upside down like a conjuring trick' (p. 198), may be a forewarning of the topsy-turvy, magical denouement to follow. Another, the overpowering presence of lilac, takes us back to an earlier incident (Chapter 2, p. 86).

Melchior, 'majestic' in a purple robe, is compared to a king or a pope (both targets of carnival parody), while Dora's thought that the robe conceals a colostomy bag reminds us of carnival's reduction of all in its reference to bodily functions.

CONTEXT

This reference to 'untimely death' serves also to remind us of the many premature demises in *Wise Children*. Grandma Chance is killed in the Blitz, Cyn's husband dies in North Africa in the war, and Cyn herself surrenders to Asian flu a few years later, while Ranulph murders his wife, Estella, and then commits suicide. Even Tiffany is presumed to have committed suicide at this point in the novel.

A further drawing in of the novel's themes and structures is the idea of life 'like a loop of tape repeating itself' (p. 199), but this too is reduced to a bodily function as the emotionally and physically bursting Dora recalls a similar meeting with her father when she did wet herself. Dora, of course, is less delicate in her choice of verb.

The meeting with Melchior (pp. 200–1) is ambiguous. Does he acknowledge them or not? Dora and Nora believe so, calling him 'Dad', but this is qualified by his playing a role before the cameras, and even his reference to 'our birthday' may be an inflated use of the royal plural. Dora can only speculate what is going on in his mind, a projection of her own thoughts more than his.

Saskia's malevolence with food is called to mind as Nora recognises one of her Italian recipes. Again, this takes us back to earlier incidents and prefigures the *Hamlet*-like action with the cake later on.

Daisy Duck's entrance is Hollywood come to London with the absurd attempt of the lutenists to have 'a go at "Hello, Dolly!"' (p. 202). People stand on chairs to glimpse the film industry's image/parody of the female form, which is brought down to earth in the fact that she is 'tight as a tick' (p. 202). However, Daisy's earthy affinity with Dora and Nora is genuine as she greets them and Lady Atalanta.

The almost relentless progression to the end of the carnival is parodied in Dora's determination that the show must go on. Tristram, supported by his aunts, makes the next entrance, and this provides Dora with the opportunity to pass appropriate comments on the appearance of the three. Tristram's reunion with his mother and father seems genuine, but this is cut short by Saskia's orchestration of the arrival of the appropriately grotesque cake in the shape of the Globe Theatre. However, the climax of the drum roll and the almost ceremonial sword for Melchior to make the first cut is **melodramatically** upstaged by a tremendous knocking at the door, Carter's punctuating signal for something about to happen: 'Something unscripted' (p. 206). This is an invitation to the reader to anticipate the next arrival and consider who could be missing.

See **Text 3** of **Extended commentaries** for further discussion of part of this section.

CONTEXT

The Globe was a theatre in Southwark, London, erected in 1599. Shakespeare had a share in the theatre, and many of his plays were first performed here. In 1613 it caught fire during a performance of Shakespeare's *Henry VIII* and was destroyed. In 1989 the site of the original Globe was rediscovered, and a reconstruction was opened in 1997.

> ### GLOSSARY
>
> | | |
> |---|---|
> | 196 | **Old Bushmills** brand of Irish whiskey |
> | 198 | **acanthus** plant with prickly leaves |
> | 199 | **'Semper Dowland, semper dolens'** (Forever Dowland, forever sad) composition by John Dowland (1563–1626), lutenist and composer; the phrase sums up his tragic view of pain and death |
> | | **'Lachrymae'** literally means 'tears'; another Dowland composition |
> | 200 | **dirndl** full, wide skirt |
> | 201 | **Canova** (1757–1822) Italian neoclassical sculptor |
> | 202 | **Bechstein** (1826–1900) German piano maker |
> | 203 | **Jean-Paul Gaulthier** Jean-Paul Gaultier (1952–), French fashion designer |
> | 204 | **Jean Muir** (1928–95) fashion designer |
> | 205 | **Italia Conte School** school for theatre arts |

PAGES 206–32

- Peregrine unexpectedly returns from South America.
- He unveils and announces Wheelchair as Lady Atalanta Hazard, then produces Tiffany from a trunk.
- The truth about the fatherhood of the four daughters is revealed.
- Dora makes love with Peregrine in the master bedroom.
- Peregrine produces the baby twins, who are taken in by Dora and Nora.
- They return to Bard Road in the early hours singing and dancing.

CONTEXT

'Finnegan's Wake' is the title of a popular comic Irish folk song of the 1850s, on which James Joyce (1882–1941) based his work *Finnegans Wake* (1939), a novel featuring complex **narrative** and **parody**. At his wake, the apparently dead Tim Finnegan is revived by the liquor splashing over him.

The door bursts open. To the singing of 'Finnegan's Wake' with its line 'Thunder and lightning! … Did yez think I was dead?' Peregrine makes his magnificent entry (p. 206). He is surrounded by numerous butterflies, and declares he has named a butterfly for 'All our daughters' and even one for Melchior.

Peregrine greets Nora and Dora, and Dora is stirred by romantic memories. Saskia remains cool and aloof; Imogen's goldfish is tipped from the bowl on her head and there is a diversion. Peregrine spots Lady Atalanta/Wheelchair. He greets her, turns her to face the crowd and announces her in the old style: 'the Lady Atalanta Hazard. The most beautiful woman of her time' (p. 209). Melchior recognises his first wife.

Peregrine now produces Tiffany from a trunk carried in by Brazilian porters. Tristram declares his love for her and asks for forgiveness, but Tiffany brusquely rejects him and his offer of marriage, advising him to marry his aunt instead. Bren and Leroy, Tiffany's parents, arrive in search of their daughter; and Tiffany leaves with them. Peregrine reveals that he had found Tiffany wandering in the street the previous night. Dora wonders if he made love to her, but Peregrine denies this.

Tristram's mother offers her son a piece of the birthday cake, but Saskia with a shriek knocks it away, and later confesses to having slipped something into the cake. In the ensuing chaos Saskia accuses Melchior of never having loved his daughters, but Dora blurts out the punchline of Gorgeous George: 'Don't worry, darlin', 'e's not your father!' (p. 213). Silence falls for a moment, and then there is pandemonium.

Lady Atalanta now reveals the Hazard family secrets, including Melchior's fathering of Dora and Nora. Peregrine announces that he is the father of Saskia and Imogen. Saskia and Imogen beg forgiveness from Lady Atalanta. Daisy gets the man accompanying her to sing, and it is only now that Dora recognises him as Puck from *The Dream*. There are tears all round.

Nora dances with her father, just as Dora had done on their seventeenth birthday. Peregrine asks Dora to dance, but she invites him to make love. Dora half recalls a previous similar occasion. Their lovemaking in the master bedroom causes the chandeliers below to shiver, and Nora suggests later that the ceiling was almost ready to collapse. During the lovemaking Dora's thoughts run through past lovers until she remembers that day in Brighton, at the age of thirteen, when it appears Peregrine first seduced her.

CHECK THE NET

To read an online version of the song 'Finnegan's Wake', visit **www.thebards.net** and click on 'Celtic Lyrics'.

CONTEXT

In an interview with Lorna Sage, Carter commented on the restricted power of carnival, stating that carnivals permit participants to get rid of the subconscious desires that they keep under control for most of the time, and that this is 'exactly what carnivals are for. The carnival has to stop. The whole point about the Feast of Fools is that things went on as they did before, after it stopped' (in *New Writing*, edited by Malcolm Bradbury and Judith Cooke, 1992).

Peregrine declares life to be a carnival, but Dora realises that reality must be faced. She suddenly wonders if Peregrine could be her father. Peregrine laughingly says this is not so, but asks her to consider who her mother could have been. He suggests that it could have been Grandma Chance. There are possibilities but no certainty in this matter.

Before they go downstairs, Dora searches the room and finds a picture of Ranulph wearing a purple robe and crown; Melchior on his hundredth birthday is wearing the 'costume of his father' (p. 224). Dora suddenly realises the problems Melchior had had to face when he was only ten years old. Peregrine finds the cardboard crown and recalls the night he teased Melchior with it.

Downstairs only the Hazard family are left. Dora places the crown on a cushion and Peregrine announces that the 'Prince of players' should reclaim his crown (p. 226). Melchior accepts it and calls Dora and Nora his 'two dancing princesses'. They feel a part of the Hazard family at last.

Peregrine invites Nora first and then Dora to feel in his pockets. They each extract a child. Twins, they are three months old, 'Brown as a quail', and supposedly the children of Gareth (p. 226). Nora and Dora will bring the twins up as their new family.

Peregrine invites Tristram to return to South America to search for Gareth; he agrees. As Nora and Dora walk back to Bard Road, pushing the twins in the Hazard baby carriage, they consider parentage. As both mothers and fathers of the babies, they believe the little twins will be wise children. Recalling the singing and dancing on their day of birth, they resolve to continue according to their lifelong maxim: 'What a joy it is to dance and sing!' (p. 232).

COMMENTARY

Peregrine's entrance has all the elements of carnival about it in every respect. It is loud, magical, mocking, upstaging, topsy-turvy in appearance. In its effects it achieves the changing, destructive, regenerative spirit of carnival before being eventually constrained within a real context.

Peregrine's dramatic entrance is heralded by words from the song 'Finnegan's Wake'. Dora claims that they sang the song about Michael Finnegan, but this is a different song – 'There was an old man called Michael Finnegan' – which repeats itself ad infinitum with its last line 'Begin again'. Either Dora or Perry and Irish have confused the name. In a way, both songs are appropriate at this juncture – a man apparently returning from the dead, the idea of things beginning again, as well as the recollection of Peregrine's raucous songs with Irish.

Huger than ever for his final reappearance, and magically surrounded by butterflies, Peregrine upstages his brother once again. Dora guides the reader to the suspension of disbelief as he upstages reality. His similarities in spirit to Dora are clear (p. 208), and the sexual overtones prepare us for a delightfully grotesque bedroom scene. His greeting to Lady Atalanta is pure Humphrey Bogart. Overt references to conjuring lead him into his production of Tiffany from a trunk. The walking carnival has come to town.

Tiffany's return, however, is important to a major theme of the novel – patriarchalism. She asserts female independence in her appearance ('she'd got on a pair of overalls and those big boots, Doc Marten's') and in her message specifically to Tristram that sex is only a part of being a father, though it applies to all. Her blunt suggestion to Tristram – 'Marry your auntie, instead' – scores 'A palpable hit' and causes Saskia to drop her glass (p. 211).

The mirroring of previous events is next seen in the cake scene. With echoes of earlier tamperings with food by the scheming Saskia, the offering of cake to Tristram brings about a comic distorted echo of the poisoned goblet scene in *Hamlet*. It also adds to the **carnivalesque** chaos as Perry pours water (and Imogen's goldfish) over the collapsed Saskia. What Saskia's intentions with Melchior's birthday cake were we never discover, though suggestions are offered.

The ability of comedy to challenge not just Saskia's accusation but also the whole question of paternity comes with Dora's instinctive reiteration of Gorgeous George's comic punchline: 'Don't worry,

---

CONTEXT

'A palpable hit' is a quotation from *Hamlet* ('A hit, a very palpable hit', V.2.282), here signifying the tangible reaction to Tiffany's remark concerning Saskia and Tristram. It also mirrors the moment when Tiffany wounds Tristram physically, catching him on the shin with one of her purple high heels just before she disappears, scoring 'a palpable hit'; although in this instance, Dora tells us, 'I don't think she'd intended to' (Chapter 1, p. 43).

darlin', '*e*'s not your father!' (p. 213). The carnivalesque idea of change follows as pandemonium breaks out and there comes a series of revelations, first of all from Lady Atalanta, who is rescued in her final confession by Peregrine. We are constantly reminded of the comic nature of the scene; Dora suggests that Lady Atalanta's retort – 'Oh, yes you did!' – to Melchior's denial should invite the stock pantomime response 'Oh, no I didn't!' (p. 214). Lady Atalanta's language, dignified and refined, in contrast to Dora's **narrative** comments, adds a further dimension to the dichotomy of the Hazard/Chance branches.

CHECK THE BOOK

Angela Carter said: 'In the end my ambition is rather an eighteenth-century "Enlightenment" one – to write fiction that entertains and, in a sense, instructs' (*Contemporary Writers: Angela Carter*, 1990).

While Lady Atalanta seems reconciled with her daughters, others are left feeling miserable (Melchior), frustrated (My Lady Margarine) or simply excluded (Peregrine). The identity of the tiny man accompanying Daisy is finally revealed as he sings 'Oh, my beloved father' (pp. 216–17). As Dora succinctly puts it: 'From Daisy Duck to Daisy Puck' (p. 217). The scene is described in theatrical terms as Dora imagines a non-existent curtain coming down and a short intermission.

Dora's escape upstairs with Peregrine is the ultimate in carnival excess. The hundred-year-old uncle makes love to his seventy-five-year-old niece on the bed of his brother and her father. The carnivalesque breaking down of all taboos is virtually complete with the suggestion that their lovemaking might bring the house down. The recollection by Dora that Peregrine had seduced her in Brighton when she was thirteen is never fully resolved. However, Peregrine's belief that 'Life's a carnival' is put into context by Dora (p. 222). The carnival can only go so far before we recognise reality. As Dora tells him, 'The carnival's got to stop, some time'. Peregrine's spirit cannot be quenched, however, as we see when he queries Dora's invitation to look at the news. 'News? What news?' says it all (p. 222).

Before returning downstairs, the suggestion from Dora that Perry might have been her father and the retort from Perry that Grandma Chance might have been her mother open up the whole debate about the father/mother issue. However, both of these possibilities remain vague speculation in the Hazard family closet.

The discovery in the bedroom of the portrait of Ranulph, which Melchior has imitated in his attire that evening, takes the reader back in time to the ten-year-old orphan and his desire to become, as Dora puts it, 'the father of himself' (p. 224). All that remains is for Peregrine to find the pasteboard crown, which is discovered in a hatbox. The presentation of the crown on a cushion to Melchior recalls the earlier incident after the fire, when Peregrine had teased his brother.

The concluding scene completes the carnivalesque idea of renewal. Melchior is seen as reduced in stature – 'two-dimensional' (p. 230) – and this leads his daughters to consider whether or not they have been inventing him all along. As Dora and Nora feel legitimate at last in their belated welcome into the Hazard family ('We'd finally wormed our way into the heart of the family we'd always wanted to be part of'), Peregrine produces his final act of magic. The twins are said to be the children of Gareth; Dora's irreverent suggestion is that a 'holy father' can now be added to the Hazard family tree, 'to add to the hypothetical, disputed, absent father' (p. 227).

There are a number of references in the closing pages to the suggestion of happy endings, which, together with the early references to 'once upon a time', suggest the idea of fairy tale. Dora's admission that the tale is hard to swallow is an open invitation for the reader to suspend – or otherwise – disbelief.

The final scene as Dora and Nora make their way home with the adopted twins is a mirror of their adoption by Grandma Chance. However, as the regeneration begins after the carnival, it is not an exact duality, for the twins are boy and girl, a new thing in the family. The life force of Dora and Nora is asserted, and the novel ends appropriately as it began, with singing and dancing in the street. The sense of life going full circle and beginning again is reinforced.

? QUESTION
Joyce Carol Oates asks: 'How to end such a farcical romance of twins, twins and more twins, except with the miraculous birth of yet another pair of twins, this time (for the first time in Hazard family history) a girl and a boy?' ('Comedy Is Tragedy That Happens to Other People', *New York Times Book Review*, 19 January 1992). What are your thoughts about the ending of the novel?

GLOSSARY

210	**made a pact** i.e. with the devil
	simulacrum image or representation
213	**Marina** abandoned daughter of Pericles in Shakespeare's play *Pericles*, who is later recognised by her father
	oeillade a knowing look
	Medusa one of the Gorgons, whose face was so terrible that all who looked at her turned to stone
220	**Josephine Baker** (1906–75) entertainer who adopted twelve children from all round the world, whom she called her Rainbow Tribe
229	**Beatrix Potter** (1866–1943) children's author and illustrator
230	**Oval** famous cricket ground in south London

CONTEXT

Peregrine's description of Irish as '*mon semblable, mon frère*' is a quote from the introductory poem 'Au Leuteur' to *Les Fleurs du mal* (*Flowers of Evil*) by Charles Baudelaire, a French symbolist poet (1821–67). In this work Baudelaire addresses the reader, involving him in an intimate relationship with the author. T. S. Eliot (1888–1965) uses the allusion in his poem *The Waste Land* (1922). The central idea in both Baudelaire and Eliot is that the poet is the voice of the spirit and that boredom or world-weariness forces us into weakness and fantasy.

Extended Commentaries

Text 1 – Chapter 1, pages 31–3

From 'Now, how had it come to pass' to 'That was her motto. Ours, too.'

This episode brings together for the first time Peregrine, Grandma Chance and the twins in what will be a life-long relationship of **carnivalesque** dimensions. It encompasses the spirit of the characters and presents that double view of adult/child that autobiographical **narrative** permits.

Dora's habit of posing a question and addressing the reader in the second person as 'you' draws the reader into the story and into a relationship with the narrator. That sense of the '*hypocrite lecteur*' that lies behind Perry's reference to Baudelaire in introducing his co-writer and other self, Irish ('*mon semblable, mon frère*', Chapter 3, p. 118), creates a sense of intimacy between reader and narrator.

The nature of Peregrine's arrival is conveyed in the idea that he 'popped up', rather like the demon king in pantomime, which is appropriate in the sense that there is a slightly menacing aspect beneath his carnivalesque appearance (p. 31). The emphasis, however, is largely on the 'glorious afternoon' that Peregrine seems to generate in order to make them all 'happy'. Peregrine's mystery is part of his fascination. His name suggests immediately a wanderer, which is exactly what he has been and will be throughout the novel to his final disappearance to the forests of Brazil. Where he has been since he was last seen escaping down Broadway as a ten-year-old is anyone's guess. There are wonderful stories to choose from when piecing together his past; he offers the girls alternatives ranging from a 'flophouse in El Paso' to the goldfields of Alaska. It is a 'Chinese banquet of options' (p. 31). Always holding a sense of romance and adventure, his adventures off stage fascinate the girls.

His gift as a storyteller casts some doubt over his many histories, but in the carnivalesque spirit of his portrayal we accept the tales as part of his character and his appeal. The partly convincing feature of his stories lies in the fact that others involved in his adventures are real people. The fact that Ambrose Bierce actually disappeared without trace in Mexico and could not deny Peregrine's story and the only evidence is a signed dedication in a copy of Bierce's *The Devil's Dictionary*, an iconoclastic, **ironic** rewriting of English, somehow does not seem to matter. Similarly, his being taught to juggle by W. C. Fields, the Hollywood comic film star, has just enough elements of truth in it to be actually possible: Fields was an excellent juggler, and so is Perry. His wearing of the US flying jacket and the shrapnel wound in the arm in a sling add to the image of Peregrine as a wandering adventurer.

The mutual affinity between Peregrine and Grandma Chance provides almost a surrogate husband for her, and definitely a surrogate father for the girls. The theme of paternity emerges more openly when Peregrine reveals the reason for his visit – Melchior's impending marriage. Too young to appreciate the fact that their biological father, who denies parentage, is about to marry, Dora places this into the childlike perspective of 'The pirates' father', referring to the bits of costume they were wearing at the time (p. 32). Their laughter later in the incident is similarly the unknowing laughter of children who laugh simply because adults are laughing.

Grandma's typical views and voice emerge in this incident. Her railing against old men out to destroy the youth of countries in

CHECK THE BOOK

Kate Webb comments: 'Peregrine is red and rude, a big man and, in the classic Rabelaisian manner, a boundary-buster, growing bigger all the time. To Dora and Nora he is the proverbial rich American uncle' (in 'Seriously Funny: *Wise Children*' in *Flesh and the Mirror: Essays on the Art of Angela Carter*, edited by Lorna Sage).

CONTEXT

Ambrose Bierce (1842–?1914) was an American soldier, adventurer, journalist and writer; he disappeared without trace in Mexico during the 1913 revolution. In 1906 he wrote *The Devil's Dictionary*, a dictionary which reinterprets the English language with satirical, often scandalous definitions.

CHECK THE BOOK

Joyce Carol Oates suggests that *Wise Children* 'would probably translate ... into a spirited, bawdy musical comedy-farce' ('Comedy Is Tragedy That Happens to Other People', *New York Times Book Review*, 19 January 1992).

her relief at seeing Peregrine safe is followed by her railing against Melchior. Her alliterative passion when she 'bearded the bastard in his den' is followed by the comic image of Melchior in mascara and tights, taken to further comic heights in the suggestion that this could affect his denial of parentage (p. 32). The juxtaposition of serious and comic is a feature of Dora's narrative. Grandma Chance's determined defiance in the face of Melchior's denial is summed up in her double-sided motto which concludes this scene: 'Hope for the best, expect the worst'. The fact that Dora says that it is 'Ours, too' indicates the grandmother's (not a father's) influence on the young girls.

TEXT 2 – CHAPTER 2, PAGES 103–5

From 'So there was an orgiastic aspect' to 'A miracle.'

This scene *à deux* in the panoramic, **carnivalesque** excesses of the fire brings Dora face to face with her father. Medieval carnival is suggested in the 'orgiastic aspect', the light – 'red and flickering flames' – providing a lurid dramatic effect. This prompts the thought that the revellers in costume (catalogued in typical Carter style) are 'guests at a masquerade who've all gone suddenly to hell' (p. 103). There is a sense of the normal world turned completely upside down.

Dora's distress is clear as she runs from group to group, blinded by tears in her search for Nora. Her panic is placed in sharp contrast to Melchior, whose behaviour and words throughout this incident are ludicrously incongruous. He is dragging a huge, ornate chair (a throne?) into a 'commanding' position in front of the fire. Calling for champagne, he watches, like Twelfth Night's Lord of Misrule, his house burn down from what he terms his 'own fireside'. The fact that champagne does immediately appear 'like a conjuring trick' adds a sense of magic to the carnival. The idea of a 'front-stalls view' suggests performance rather than disaster, nothing as it should be in true carnivalesque spirit (p. 104).

Melchior's colloquial 'Give us a hand' is also out of place, as too is the later exchange between him and Dora – 'Or is it Nora?' – which reminds us of his detachment from his daughters. The inconsequentiality of the conversation ends in a ludicrous anticlimax; the incongruity in the movement between the comic ('You've lost your eyebrows') and the tragic ('I've lost my sister') and back to the comic ('I've lost … my crown') creates a black humour. This reflects Carter's idea that 'Comedy is tragedy that happens to *other* people' (Chapter 5, p. 213). Dora's 'toasty warm' feeling, contrasting with her 'backside', which is 'bitter cold', is at odds too with her bitter cold spirits in her realisation that Nora is missing – a reversal of Dora's usual **bathos** in this serious moment.

Melchior, however, is performing. His monologue – almost a soliloquy – is Richard II in a mad context, a king lamenting a pasteboard crown. His contrived use of 'we mummers' and the suggestion of 'simple folk' are comically out of place (p. 105). The delivery leads up to what is for him the climax, but what is essentially for Dora and the reader a dreadful anticlimax. The pasteboard crown means more to him than 'wealth, or fame, or women, or children', a value system turned on its head. With the inflated 'Othello's occupation gone!' and tears running down his cheeks (previously 'Not the sign of a tear'), Melchior's performance invites audience response. Dora feels the urge to applaud 'the old fraud', but the scene is punctuated dramatically by exclamations which lead into the next episode in the drama. A scene of madly comic effect alongside the reality of potential tragedy has been enacted in the true spirit of carnival – a world and its values turned upside down, the 'make-believe' more important to Melchior than horrible reality.

TEXT 3 – CHAPTER 5, PAGES 196–7

From 'He stretched out his hand' to 'I felt quite revived.'

Here we have the final appearance of Gorgeous George (does he represent King George or St George?), who first was seen on Brighton Pier in his sentimental, patriotic and innuendo-strewn comic act. He was then the essence of post-war music hall, a comedian with aspects recognisable in a number of actual performers.

He is now reduced to begging in the street. Given that George is a kind of walking metaphor with his map of the world tattooed on his body, his greatly changed circumstances add a new level of

> **CONTEXT**
>
> A mummer was an actor in a mummers' play, a traditional English folk play popular in the eighteenth and early nineteenth centuries and often associated with Christmas. The plot typically featured St George and involved a miraculous resurrection. Used in a derogatory sense, a mummer is a contemptuous name for an actor.

CHECK THE FILM

In 1984 Angela Carter wrote the screenplay for *The Company of Wolves*, a **Gothic** and magical realist adaptation of stories from *The Bloody Chamber*, directed by Neil Jordan.

meaning here. Beneath a stained ex-army greatcoat (British military might diminished) the map of the world is partly visible. The pink bits of the British Empire are now faded beneath the reality of the 'harsh light of the yellow streetlamps' (p. 196). The old order has changed for all the Georges: Gorgeous George, St George and the dynasty of kings who share his name. Dora gives us an elevated Miltonic reference, 'Lo, how the mighty are fallen', **intertextuality** becoming a cheap pun in this changed context.

One of Dora's typical moments of introspection breaks up the **narrative** as she ponders 'untimely death' (p. 196). Is it Peregrine or Tiffany in her thoughts? She considers too the reason for attending this birthday party. Paternity is recognised by the 'wise child', though Melchior has never acknowledged Dora and Nora.

The beggar's blunt plea 'Give us a bob, then' returns Dora from reverie to reality. The **irony** of the twenty-pound note with its image of Shakespeare and the memory of George as Bottom in *The Dream* both conjure up the past. In a surrealistically comic moment Shakespeare speaks: 'Have a heart.' Dora's condition for the gift is typical: it is for George to spend it all on drink. Her farewell reminds us of George's link to country and empire; and it is also the rallying call from *Henry V*. She concludes with a defiant request that George should 'drink a health to bastards' (p. 197). Gorgeous George's puzzlement causes the reader to ask if she is referring to George himself, to Shakespeare's bastard characters or to herself and Nora as the bastard children of Melchior.

CONTEXT

Henry V urges his men to 'Cry "God for Harry! England and Saint George!"' (*Henry V*, III.1.34) outside the walls of Harfleur.

The moment passes as George disappears, and the girls make their spirited entrance. Self-mockery is endearingly present in the description of their 'antique but not quite catastrophic legs' and the glitz of the 'silver-fox trenches' (did Howard Hughes really give them to the girls, we half wonder?). Their style with their coats, 'trailing them behind us', is pure catwalk and produces the right response as cameras flash. Dora feels 'revived' and ready to greet Melchior.

CONTEXT

Howard Hughes (1905–76) was a millionaire businessman, film producer and director and aviator born in Houston, Texas.

The scene is at once a reminder of the past, a memento mori for Dora, a reminder of the illegitimacy issue and a revival of the old spirit in the overdressed twins. Primarily, however, this encounter with George is the final piece in the metaphorical statement of his tattooed body, the last word in the decline of empire.

PART THREE

CRITICAL APPROACHES

CHARACTERISATION

Wise Children contains a splendid array of characters, whose roles vary from major to minor players, to extras and to a host of names who have played some small part in the lives of the Hazard and Chance families.

Dora as the narrator is the major character. Her close relationships with her twin, Nora, and Grandma Chance play a large part in the early chronological life. Grandma Chance's adopted family includes not only Dora and Nora, but Cyn, who is taken in as a stray and becomes the grandmother of Brenda, who in turn is the mother of Tiffany. Dora and Nora are fascinated by their father, Melchior Hazard, who does not acknowledge them until his one hundredth birthday, when they are seventy-five years old.

Dora and Nora's involvement with their uncle, Melchior's wandering brother Peregrine, focuses the issues of parentage and legitimacy. Their adoption of Wheelchair (Lady Atalanta Hazard), the first wife of Melchior, and their antipathy to her two daughters, Saskia and Imogen, provide further focal points for developing family relationships. Tristram and Gareth, another set of twins born to Melchior's third wife, figure in the story, the former in his involvement with Tiffany, the latter as the potential father of the twins magically produced by Peregrine at the end of the novel.

In Hollywood Daisy Duck, destined to be for a brief time the second wife of Melchior, and her husband Genghis Khan, the film mogul, play short but significant roles in the girls' film careers. Along the way to fame and back to obscurity, the girls cross paths with several lovers, as well as a number of actors and writers who impinge on their lives to a greater or lesser extent. Behind these characters lurks the family history with its portrayals of Sir Ranulph Hazard and his wife Estella, and the third point of this love triangle, Cassius Booth.

 CHECK THE NET
For a comprehensive film database listing cinematic adaptations of Shakespeare, and in particular *A Midsummer Night's Dream*, search the Internet Movie Database at **www.imdb.com**

The dramatis personae (pp. 233–4) is a facetious **parody** of the credits at the end of a film, but does serve to indicate the order that the characters appear in the book, though not in the chronology of the family history.

DORA CHANCE

Dora is the narrator of the action, who tells her story in a free, irreverent tragicomic style and is, above all, a 'wise child' (Chapter 2, p. 73). She is the twin sister of Nora. The physical similarities of the sisters are responsible for their success as the Lucky Chances on stage and also for many of the disguises, illusions and mistaken identities in the plot.

Dora and her twin are illegitimate in every way: by birth, by their position on the wrong side of London – 'the *bastard* side of Old Father Thames' (Chapter 1, p. 1) – by their involvement in non-legit theatre. She seeks acknowledgement of her paternity, the legitimising of herself and her story. Her almost romantic attraction to Melchior is highlighted in a series of ephemeral older lovers. Unlike Nora, who 'each time she fell in love, she fell in love for the first time' (Chapter 2, p. 82), only once do we see Dora truly fall in love, and **ironically** it is with Nora's boyfriend. When she meets her young tenor again, at the party at Melchior's house, she says: 'To die for love runs in the family … And that night was the one time in all my life I thought that such a thing might be worth while' (Chapter 2, p. 100). The young tenor aside, her romantic descriptions are invariably reserved for her father and her uncle; Dora's heart goes 'pit-a-pat' when she sees Melchior at her seventeenth birthday party (Chapter 2, p. 87), and she describes her feelings when he is near her as being an 'indigestible mix of … joy, terror, heartsick, lovesick' (Chapter 4, p. 172). As for Peregrine, we are left in doubt as to whether or not she was seduced by him when she was only thirteen.

Dora's **voice** has a similar blend of the refined and the profane shown by Grandma Chance, who has brought her up. Her literary style also has the voice of the real Dora and a literate voice, perhaps taught to her by Irish. She also has a reflective view of life, which emerges in the telling of the story.

CONTEXT

Dora was the pseudonym given to Ida Bauer (1882–1945), one of Sigmund Freud's patients. She was sent to him in 1900 suffering from 'hysterical' symptoms, having been abused by her father.

CHECK THE BOOK

Kate Webb comments: 'Nor is Dora's name accidental. In another example of "writing back", Carter's Dora, unlike her Freudian namesake, suffers very little psychic damage from lusting after her father … or her uncle' (see p. 293 of 'Seriously Funny: *Wise Children*' in *Flesh and the Mirror: Essays on the Art of Angela Carter*, edited by Lorna Sage).

Her theatrical career traces English non-legitimate strands from pantomime to music hall, to brief fame in the West End of London and Hollywood, to the demise of music hall in nude revues. Her philosophy is 'What a joy it is to dance and sing!' (Chapter 1, p. 34), a philosophy which guides her to the end of the story.

Dora possesses the warmth and humanity of Grandma Chance. This is shown in the 'adoption' of Lady Atalanta Hazard, Melchior's first wife, who is promptly named Wheelchair in irreverent acknowledgement of her new life. The adoption of the new twins brings joy to the seventy-five-year-old twins at the end of the novel, when, in true Grandma Chance style, they return to Bard Road with a new family.

NORA CHANCE

Nora is the twin sister of Dora, identical but not symmetrical. Though in terms of career and the romantic attraction of the distant Melchior all that is said of Dora applies to Nora, she is different in many ways. Dora tells the reader early on that her sister 'said "Yes!" to life and I said, "Maybe ..."' (Chapter 1, p. 5). Their very different attitudes to love highlight the differences in their characters. Nora's readiness to throw herself into love affairs, holding nothing back ('Nora ... threw her heart away as if it were a used bus ticket', Chapter 2, p. 80), provides her with a steady stream of men, and contrasts with Dora's more reserved, hesitant attitude ('The more I saw of love, the less I liked the look of it', Chapter 2, p. 82).

Fittingly, it is Nora who loses her virginity first, and Nora who gets married, albeit for an extremely brief time. Her intention to convert to the Roman Catholic faith in order to marry Tony hints at her desire for a family and children of her own – more than once Dora tells us of Nora's desire to be a mother, and her reaction to the appearance of the twins at the climax of the novel is powerful. Dora notes her sister's reaction as she feels the baby in Peregrine's pocket: 'She looked as if she were about to fall in love ... terminally' (Chapter 5, p. 226); and on their way home Dora describes the 'heart-shaped glow' that seems to surround Nora as she pushes the pram (Chapter 5, p. 229).

www. CHECK THE NET

S. L. Deefholts states that Dora and Nora are 'metaphorical mirror images, in the sense that they are inversions of each other' (in 'Hazarding Chance: Reading Angela Carter's *Wise Children*'). See p. 63 of these Notes for details of how to find this article online.

Providing a mirror image to Dora, Nora takes part in a number of disguises, one of which is the sharing of an early lover for Dora's first sexual experience. This episode serves to illustrate not only their unselfish love for one another, a love which overrides all others (when Dora fears Nora has died in the fire at Melchior's house she admits: 'To tell the truth, I love her best and always have', Chapter 2, p. 102), but also emphasises their different personalities. Nora manages to keep up the identity switch for a while, but after a couple of drinks 'carried on in her usual fashion' and 'started dancing on the table' (Chapter 2, p. 84). Not only does the more outgoing Nora provide Dora with her first lover, but her behaviour that night supplies her with her second, Mr Piano Man.

From the moment of their birth their lives are intertwined, and Nora shares with Dora the joy of new life and the ability to continue to sing and dance, if not on stage then in real life.

GRANDMA CHANCE

CHECK THE BOOK
Carter portrays various mothers as well as fathers in *Wise Children*. Nicole Ward Jouve points out that 'the Hazard girls, none of them biological mothers, do some excellent mothering', and it is Grandma Chance who 'whether she was their biological mother or not, has made the girls feel safe as houses' ('"Mother is a Figure of Speech"', p. 157, in *Flesh and the Mirror: Essays on the Art of Angela Carter*, edited by Lorna Sage).

Grandma Chance seems to have invented herself as well as her adopted family. She appears almost by chance on a New Year's Day and sets up home in Bard Road. Generous in spirit and heart, she takes in Dora and Nora, twins born to Kitty the young servant girl, who dies in childbirth. She also takes in a young waif who mysteriously appears at the door with a note from Peregrine. The stray, in true family tradition, becomes Our Cyn, grandmother to Brenda, who in turn gives birth to Tiffany.

Grandma's south London blend of mock refinement and downright profanity sets her character. Her motto 'Hope for the best, expect the worst' is her philosophy on life. Her affinity with Peregrine, a consequence of their carnival spirit, their *joie de vivre* and their humanity, is apparent each time they meet. Grandma is the influential and protective matriarchal figure, the opposite to the ineffectual and absent patriarchal figures in the story. She is the archivist for the Lucky Chances' stage career, keeping programmes, scrapbooks and costumes. Her death on her way to the off-licence in the London Blitz has an appropriately tragicomic touch in the light of her motto. Beneath it all, however, her loss is felt deeply by Dora and Nora; but, in true Grandma Chance spirit, life must go on.

Her final 'appearance' in the story is more of a manifestation as her distinctive toque falls from the wardrobe, followed by an avalanche of gloves and clothes. Long dead, she seems to speak to Dora and Nora with her familiar message to seize the day.

MELCHIOR HAZARD

Melchior is the son of Sir Ranulph Hazard, the great Shakespearian actor-manager, who took Shakespeare to the world in his travelling shows. The deaths of his parents in a love triangle tragedy leave him and his twin brother orphaned at the age of ten. In the Hazard family tradition, Melchior is unlike his twin, Peregrine, in many ways.

Melchior becomes the patriarchal figurehead of the Hazard family and English theatre. He is three times married, firstly to Lady Atalanta Lynde (later Wheelchair), secondly to Daisy Duck (Delia Delaney), and finally to My Lady Margarine, the anonymous best friend of Saskia who played Cordelia to Melchior's Lear. He is the father of twins Saskia and Imogen by Lady Atalanta, and Tristram and Gareth by My Lady Margarine, though the true paternity of both sets remains doubtful to the end. He is the father of the illegitimate twins Dora and Nora, who are brought up by Grandma Chance.

The name Melchior may have some significance as it is the name of one of the three kings, the Magi, or wise men, in the Nativity story. The idea of Melchior as a king runs through the novel: he is a king of sorts in his family, the king of English theatre, a player of kings in Shakespeare – all roles which sometimes cross over from the real to the illusory. Judgement about his wisdom clearly lies in the gypsy's warning and his relationships, in both senses of the word, with his children.

Running away 'to seek his forture like Dick Whittington in panto', he rises to fame in Shakespearian roles. On his way to the top, he fathers Dora and Nora, their mother a servant in the house of Grandma Chance. She dies in childbirth and Melchior denies parentage. His ambitions in England realised, his hopes to conquer America lie in the missionary zeal he inherits from his father. He is self-centred in his ambitions and patriarchal in his attitudes to

CHECK THE BOOK

Referring to Melchior's cardboard crown, Aidan Day writes: 'The token of kingly authority to which Melchior adhered was a bit of cardboard, a sham, just like his outward show of pure cultural legitimacy' (*Angela Carter: The Rational Glass*, 1998).

CHECK THE FILM

Adrian Noble's 1996 film of *A Midsummer Night's Dream*, based on his Royal Shakespeare Company production of the play, is worth watching for its innovative and somewhat eccentric design. The forest is a sea of floating light bulbs; Titania's bower in which she seduces Bottom is a giant umbrella.

family and those he meets in the theatre. In later life he is reduced to appearances in television adverts and a bewildered guest appearance on Tristram's game show.

He is frequently upstaged in many ways by his brother, Peregrine, for example at his own birthday party when Peregrine, thought to be long dead, bursts in and steals Melchior's thunder. Several incidents illustrate the differences in character and the rivalry that exists between them.

On his hundredth birthday, a day he and Peregrine share with Melchior's illegitimate daughters Nora and Dora, as well as Shakespeare, Melchior is made to face the truth about the secrets in the Hazard family closet.

PEREGRINE HAZARD

Peregrine is the twin brother of Melchior, offspring of Sir Ranulph and Estella Hazard. Peregrine is the spirit of carnival that runs through the book. True to his name, he is a wanderer, a pilgrim appearing and disappearing suddenly. His wanderings and mysterious, adventurous, improbable life begin at the age of ten, when he runs off from his Presbyterian aunt and vanishes 'clean away into America' (Chapter 1, p. 22). The stories he tells of his early years in America set the tone for this man who plays many roles. He is in turn boy actor, runaway, soldier, airman, actor, magician, conjuror, gold prospector, rancher, sheriff, oilman, financial investor on Wall Street, explorer, scriptwriter, impresario, something in the secret service, lepidopterist. He seduces with his many histories and he also seduces women. Exactly how many of these careers he actually had is never certain.

The mystery extends to exactly how far he is involved with Hazard and Chance family affairs. Did he seduce Dora at thirteen? Could he have been the father of Dora and Nora by Grandma Chance, or by Kitty for that matter? He is said to be the father of Imogen and Saskia, and could also be the father of Tristram and Gareth. The exact answers to most of Peregrine's wanderings in the world or through the bedrooms of the Hazard family are never fully revealed.

Whenever Peregrine appears, always at critical points in the story, he seems to grow larger and more exuberant than before. He is generous to Dora and Nora, acting as a surrogate father and providing them and Grandma Chance with money and presents which delight them. At times, however, Peregrine can be seen as a slightly menacing figure, not unlike the big bad wolf of fairy tale.

'Life's a carnival' is Peregrine's motto (Chapter 5, p. 222). Certainly in carnival spirit he brings life and a huge, exaggerated exuberant magic to his visits. In his final appearance, dramatically heralded by a huge wind that seems to blow through the whole room, he is surrounded by dozens of butterflies. 'The size of a warehouse, bigger, the size of a tower block' (Chapter 5, p. 206), he upstages his brother once again, magically produces Tiffany from a trunk, makes loud and riotous love to Dora on Melchior's bed and rediscovers Melchior's crown – in short, virtually takes over and runs the show.

In the end, however, he does not really belong. He contemplates the outcome if he were to continue the carnival, but Dora reminds him, not entirely successfully, that the carnival must acknowledge reality. The carnival, as Dora tells him, must end at some point, or there will be chaos. It is not just that this life does not seem to be able to contain him, but ultimately he is rejected by his daughters, Saskia and Imogen. He returns to Brazil, his study of butterflies and the search for Gareth.

CHECK THE BOOK

In his introduction to *Burning Your Boats* (1995), Salman Rushdie says: 'Carter's other country is the fairground, the world of the gimcrack showman, the hypnotist, the trickster, the puppeteer.' Both Peregrine and Melchior belong in many ways to this world of illusion.

LADY ATALANTA HAZARD (WHEELCHAIR)

'The most beautiful woman of her time', at the end of the story Lady Atalanta's eyes still retain some of that beauty. She is the first wife of Melchior Hazard, 'a proper lady', with title, wealth and lands. Her rejection by Melchior for Daisy Duck is accepted with typical dignity. Even in reduced circumstances she remains happy with her lot and loyal to the memory of Melchior in the cold surroundings of Lynde Court Home Farm.

Indeed, this dignity is the quality she shows throughout, though she is shown little respect in the way Dora and Nora speak to her; frequently they refer to her as an object. As Wheelchair she is often plugged in (to the television), greased (with bacon) – in short treated like a machine. Dora describes her distress at the fate of Tiffany as 'a whoosh of rubber tyres' (Chapter 1, p. 50). However, in terms of actual treatment it is Dora and Nora who take her in, who look after her, partly in recognition, Dora reveals, of Lady Atalanta's kindness to them over the years. Beginning with her early gift of forget-me-nots to the twins when they are in pantomine in Kennington, Lady Atalanta over the ensuing decades never fails to acknowledge Dora and Nora and include them in Hazard family occasions, such as Saskia and Imogen's twenty-first birthday party. In the chaos that is unleashed following Daisy's announcement of her pregnancy, Lady Atalanta still manages to greet Dora and Nora with warmth, and Dora says: 'And that's another reason we took the old trout in, because she gave us a hug and kissed us … as if we were family' (Chapter 3, p. 148).

In Bard Road she bears some resemblance to Grandma Chance, losing some of her refinement and gaining an ability to shock the local tradesmen ('Have you got anything in the shape of a cucumber, my good fellow?'). Her recognition at the end by Peregrine with his greeting of 'bright eyes' (Chapter 5, p. 209) reminds us of her beauty and also of her brief affair with him, resulting in the births of Saskia and Imogen.

SASKIA HAZARD

CONTEXT

Starring in one of Melchior's productions, Saskia plays one of the witches in *Macbeth*. While Dora snidely comments 'typecasting' (Chapter 4, p. 171), it might be more apt to draw parallels between Saskia and Lady Macbeth.

Saskia is the scheming, predatory half of the Hazard twins from Melchior's first marriage to Lady Atalanta. She is the antithesis of her sister, Imogen. Her proclivity for doctoring food to suit her own ends, either in revenge or in a devious attempt to gain sexually or financially, is just one unpleasant aspect of her character. Others are her treatment of Lady Atalanta – her appropriation of her money and possessions and her abandonment of her mother after the fall, indirectly caused by her in the first place – and her seduction of Tristram, her half-brother by her father's third marriage, to gain revenge on Melchior for marrying her best friend.

Her selfishness places her at the opposite end of the spectrum to Dora with her altruism; and the antipathy between the two is apparent at each meeting. Dora refers to her as her '*bête noire*' (Chapter 1, p. 38) and 'a cold-blooded cow' (Chapter 5, p. 205),

among other barbed descriptions. Saskia's father turns out to be
Peregrine, but she rejects him and clings to Melchior, who probably
offers more in terms of financial security, if not love.

IMOGEN HAZARD

Imogen's claim to fame is her role as Goldie the Goldfish on a
children's programme. The sister of Saskia, she is the complete
opposite, being docile, indolent and imitative in a pale way. Her
reaction to Dora and Nora's first pantomine performance neatly
sums up her future personality: she 'fell asleep and left her mouth
open' (Chapter 1, p. 77). Her appearance with a goldfish in a bowl
on her head is a magical realist attempt to show her true calibre;
Dora tells the reader that 'she was always a strange one' (Chapter 5,
p. 229). The rest is silence, as Dora might say.

MY LADY MARGARINE

She is the third and much younger wife of Melchior, and mother
to Tristram and Gareth, though the hints about Peregrine's calls
to Gunter Grove suggest that he may have had a hand in their
conception. Her marriage to Melchior has its roots in their King
Lear and Cordelia roles, and replicates the marriage of Ranulph
and Estella, Melchior's parents. Saskia's best friend at RADA, her
talents in later life lie in television advertising, hence the nickname
Dora gives her. In real life she is pretty much ineffectual, as shown
in the final crisis scenes of revelation. She is referred to throughout
as My Lady Margarine, Numero Tre, or 'the girl who, once upon a
time, played Cordelia to our father's Lear' (Chapter 1, p. 37). We
never learn her name.

 CHECK THE NET

Visit
**www.en.thinkexist.
com** for a wide
range of quotations
from Carter that
give insights into
her views on fiction
and her writing.
Go to 'Authors';
names are listed
alphabetically by
first names.

TRISTRAM HAZARD

Tristram is the son of Melchior and My Lady Margarine, though
doubts about his parentage make him a typical Hazard offspring.
He is the twin brother of Gareth, although he bears little
resemblance to him in character and appearance, another Hazard
trait. His shallowness is seen in the role he plays on television as
host of a quiz show with mercenary overtones. It is also apparent
in his treatment of Tiffany, as he keeps several casual lovers,
remains faithful to his incestuous affair with Saskia and rejects
Tiffany when he discovers she is pregnant. His embarrassment

in front of a live television audience is exquisitely acute. His later pathetic attempts to win her back and be a father to the child are rejected by the emancipated Tiffany. He disappears at the end, going to South America with Peregrine in search for Gareth.

GARETH HAZARD

He is the twin brother of Tristram, offspring of Melchior and My Lady Margarine. A Jesuit missionary, he seems the opposite of Tristram the playboy. His missionary zeal is channelled towards converting the unfaithful, not towards the theatre like the rest of the Hazard dynasty. However, something of the Hazard zeal for procreation must exist in him, if we believe Peregrine when he says that Gareth has fathered twins in South America. And, true to his Hazard roots, he abandons them.

GENGHIS KHAN

> **CONTEXT**
>
> Genghis Khan (1162–1227) was a powerful Mongol warrior and conqueror. Born Temujin, he later changed his name to Genghis Khan, meaning 'Universal Ruler', and by the time of his death the Mongol empire stretched from the Black Sea to the Pacific.

This is the name that Dora gives the American film producer of *The Dream*. We never learn his real name, and even his first wife is referred to as Mrs Genghis Khan. The name, like others in the novel, is appropriate, for he is a tyrant and displays some sadistic qualities. He is dictatorial in the film kingdom (which Dora describes as being the size of Monaco) that he rules over. His jodhpurs and whip (used on one occasion to silence Puck) are comically indicative of his despotism and in some ways recall archetypical images of the Hollywood mogul. His worse than patriarchal attitude to women is seen in his treatment of budding young stars, and the wooing, proposal and 'marriage' to Dora is as abrupt as it is convenient. His enjoyment in feeding his carnivorous plants suggests deeper complexities of cruelty. The **irony** of his remarriage to his disguised first wife who has pursued him throughout seems to be dispelled in the knowledge that they seem happy together, 'once he'd got over the shock', although Dora suggests that 'if you believe that, you'll believe anything' (Chapter 3, p. 161).

DAISY DUCK (DELIA DELANEY)

Daisy is the second wife of Genghis Khan, having risen from relative obscurity to fame like so many Hollywood stars. She is unashamedly brash, and in dress and mannerisms and the double alliteration of her adopted name Delia Delaney she reminds the reader of other Hollywood actresses. Her first words on seeing Dora and Nora in her apartment with Peregrine are to ask when the orgy is; her first action is to throw a telephone from the window. She, like Dora and Nora, has spent a lifetime in entertainment, rising to stardom through talent shows, early films as a child star, the Mack Sennett bathing belle films and subsequent singing and dancing roles in Hollywood. Her later stardom is attributed to her ability to play a certain role, the 'classic thirties blonde', whose qualities she seems to have naturally – 'tough, sweet, lewd, funny, fast, tender' (Chapter 3, p. 115). Despite her lack of class, these qualities, more than reminiscent of Dora herself, create an instant attraction.

> **CONTEXT**
>
> Mack Sennett (1880–1960) was an American film-maker, particularly of comedies featuring, amongst others, Charlie Chaplin, the Keystone Kops and, later, the Bathing Beauties.

Daisy is won over by Melchior in the rehearsals for *The Dream*. However, her marriage to Melchior is quickly annulled when it becomes clear that she is not pregnant, and she ultimately marries the undersized, oversexed actor who played Puck. She reappears at Melchior's one hundredth birthday party and makes a grand entrance to music and cheers, despite being 'half seas over' (Chapter 5, p. 202).

IRISH (ROSS O'FLAHERTY)

A hard-drinking, boisterous Irish writer, Irish is for a brief spell the lover and educator of Dora (Dora notes how Irish is simultaneously 'Attracted … to my conspicuous unrefinement' and distressed at 'how vulgar I could be'). His disillusionment with having to sell his art to Hollywood is apparent. Dora is introduced to him by Peregrine, who describes him as '*mon semblable, mon frère*' (Chapter 3, p. 118). He collaborates with Peregrine on the script of *The Dream*. His tuition of Dora in English and the great works of literature accounts in part for the literary **allusions** in her text and some elements of style.

Final glimpses of Irish show him in the grip of alcoholism, collapsing or near to collapse and eventually near to death. However, he does receive the Pulitzer Prize posthumously for his book *Hollywood Elegies*, which indicates his quality as a writer. His portrayal of Dora may be partly accurate but it is barbed and may be caused, to some extent, by her rejection of him.

THEMES

LEGITIMACY AND NON-LEGITIMACY

This theme is explored in three senses in the novel:

- Dora and Nora's quest for legitimacy within the Hazard family.

- The legitimate world of theatre and high culture in contrast to the non-legitimate world of music hall and low culture.

- The legitimacy of Dora's story as a work of literature.

Unaware of the question of paternity until their father is pointed out dramatically by Grandma Chance in the theatre, Dora becomes from that moment acutely aware of their absent father. His rejections of the twins as his daughters in the dressing room at the Brighton theatre, at his Twelfth Night party and in his opening speech for *The Dream* leave them on the outside. In the first instance they are nieces; in the second less valuable than a cardboard crown; in the third nieces again, **ironically** this time 'almost as precious to me as my own daughters' and named by their roles as Peaseblossom and Mustardseed. When he addresses them by their real names, he gets them muddled up – 'He didn't even know us well enough to smell the difference' (Chapter 3, p. 134). At the first rejection Peregrine presents Melchior with the warning that holds the title of the novel: 'It's a wise child that knows its own father', following this with the meaningful 'But wiser yet the father who knows his own child' (Chapter 2, p. 73). Melchior's wisdom is in question here and even his eventual realisation and acknowledgement owe more to sentiment and inevitability than wisdom. Tiffany's warning to Tristram about there being more to fathering than the act of sex applies just as much to Melchior, and possibly also to Peregrine.

Nora and Dora's defiance in the face of their illegitimacy is clear throughout the story. They are 'the offspring of the bastard king' (Chapter 2, p. 67), which could be more than just an acknowledgement of their situation: perhaps a comment on the father who refuses to acknowledge them, perhaps a comment on his own paternity, of which there is some doubt, perhaps a comment on the kingly roles he assumes on and off the stage. The conflict

> **? QUESTION**
> In Greek mythology Oedipus unwittingly killed his father and married his mother. In Freudian theory the Oedipus complex refers to a child's unconscious sexual desire for the parent of the opposite sex and wish to exclude the parent of the same sex. What examples of incestuous or Oedipal relationships can you find in *Wise Children*?

of physical legitimacy produces the rivalry between the legitimate Saskia and Imogen and the illegitimate Dora and Nora; but this too is turned topsy-turvy, when the situation is turned on them.

The conflict between high and low culture is made clear from the outset: 'our father was a pillar of the legit. theatre and we girls are illegitimate in every way – not only born out of wedlock, but we went on the halls, didn't we!' (Chapter 1, p. 11). It is reinforced when, as thirteen-year-olds, they stand outside the theatre in Brighton 'looking at the glossy photos of Father togged up in a kilt' as he treads 'the boards like billy-ho, in Shakespeare, and weren't we fresh from singing in the streets?' (Chapter 2, p. 69). Though the success of high culture for a time places Melchior on a pedestal as the king of English theatre and relegates the music hall and Nora and Dora to nude revue, the situation is later reversed, subverted by the emergence of a new low culture: television. The fact that Melchior is reduced to playing his part in this low culture's adverts adds to the subversion.

Melchior's failure to emulate his father, Ranulph, in taking Shakespeare to the colonies, albeit by now an independent union of states, is a defeat for his version of high culture in the face of low culture represented by Hollywood. Melchior sees his battle to conquer Hollywood as 'Shakespeare's revenge for the War of Independence' (Chapter 3, p. 148), 'his chance to take North America back for England, Shakespeare and St George' (Chapter 3, p. 133).

Legitimacy of art is also apparent in Dora's own story. The intention to write her **memoirs**, create order out of the collected data of the Chance and the Hazard families in the 'archaeology' of her desk, becomes in the end a novel. Thus, in spite of the many bastardisings from Shakespeare and other writers, the **carnivalesque** plots and the story's refusal to remain in one time or place, Dora asserts her legitimacy in the art of the novel. The reversal of Irish's predicament is another carnivalesque feature in the subversion of normal order. In a different way from the drawing of Irish into the '*mon semblable, mon frère*' relationship, in which Irish must prostitute his art to low culture, Dora moves

> **CONTEXT**
>
> Salman Rushdie describes Angela Carter as 'a thumber of noses, a defiler of sacred cows. She loved nothing so much as cussed – but also blithe – nonconformity. Her books unshackle us, toppling the statues of the pompous, demolishing the temples ... of righteousness ... from all that is unrighteous, illegitimate, low' ('Angela Carter, 1940–92: A Very Good Wizard, a Very Dear Friend', *New York Times Book Review*, 8 March 1992).

> **CONTEXT**
>
> The War of Independence (1775–83) was the name given to the revolt of the American colonies against British rule, which culminated in the formation of the United States of America.

from the low culture of theatre to her role as a novelist. Whether we believe the story or not is not the issue. Dora, in her drawing of the reader into Baudelaire's intimacy with the writer, has given us the chance to disbelieve. The incredibility of carnivalesque scenes, extraordinary characters and the fabulous alongside the real are all held within Dora's creation. Years on the non-legit side as a hoofer 'pounding the boards' are rewarded in her emergence as a legitimate novelist. This comes just after the acknowledgement of her parentage and rightful position in the Hazard family.

PATRIARCHALISM

Angela Carter's deflating of the myth of male dominance, replacing it with a different order based on female qualities of love, appears many times in her novels and stories. In the search for legitimate identity, Melchior is brought to the fore. His denial of his illegitimate children is mirrored by Tristram's refusal to accept Tiffany's pregnancy. Tiffany's blunt advice to Tristram (Chapter 5, p. 211) serves also as a warning to patriarchal attitudes that hold the belief that the male can control matters.

Melchior's patriarchal attitude extends to his marriages, his role in society as king of British theatre and lord over the 'English Colony' in Hollywood, and his Shakespearian roles as king, be it of human or fairy worlds. Perhaps the world of Shakespeare overlaps seamlessly into his real world. The converse could also be said to be true, for in the kingdom of Oberon male rule is dominant, just as it is in Athens, and just as it is in Genghis's Hollywood kingdom.

The role that Melchior has assigned to himself in life is placed into its full context at the end of the novel. Though his pasteboard crown is mocked by Peregrine in the fire scene, its presence in Melchior's closet alongside the portrait of Ranulph in a purple robe asks the reader to reconsider his position. His patriarchal arrogance and selfishness are softened by an understanding of the childhood influence that shaped his life. In the end he seems deflated, 'two-dimensional', as Dora puts it, 'one of those great, big, papier-mâché heads ... larger than life, but not lifelike'. Nora expresses the thought that they might have made up this figure, 'a collection of our hopes and dreams and wishful thinking' (Chapter 5, p. 230). It is as if in carnival spirit he has been dethroned.

CONTEXT

Frequently when Melchior speaks, it is possible to detect the world of Shakespeare entering his speech. This is most vividly apparent in his important declamations: while watching his house burn, at Saskia and Imogen's twenty-first birthday party, at the close of filming of *The Dream* and at his one hundredth birthday celebrations.

Male dominance is subverted elsewhere. Genghis's return to his first wife is stage-managed by Dora. Even Peregrine's **carnivalesque** but male role as puller of strings is overthrown at the end; for the first time in the novel he appears lost and alone. He returns to Brazil with Tristram, another male put in his place by female assertion, in this case Tiffany's. The corollary of patriarchalism in families in the context of *Wise Children* is the Grandma-dominated household in Bard Road. In Grandma Chance's invented family there is a different regime based on adoption, love and true romance. Dora and Nora's emergence in the final scenes as continuing this regime (as perhaps they have already done with Wheelchair) is meant to be seen as a triumph of a female order over male dominance, which has proved unacceptable. In a **postmodernist** sense, Dora and Nora, the female protagonists, subvert male-dominant authority and through a continuing carnivalesque spirit look to the future as heads of their own family of twins. The regeneration is complete and a sense of something different is present. For the first time, the twins are male and female.

DECLINE OF EMPIRE AND TRADITION

The story of Dora and Nora is a journey through the changing times of the twentieth century which, while it is not a socio-historical survey, does chart changes in many aspects of life, not least the ones closest to the twins – the world of entertainment. The pattern of change, from thriving live theatre to Hollywood, to the split between high and low culture, the former enjoying success with the music halls declining and then the subsequent rise to prominence of low culture, exemplified in *Wise Children* by Tristram's dreadful television game show, is chartered in Dora's **memoirs**.

A further change was the emergence in the fifties and sixties of independent nations within a Commonwealth. The decline of the British Empire meant that Britain's role and image were changing. Gorgeous George charts not only the decline of the music hall but, with his tattoo of a map of the world, he is a walking metaphor for the decline of empire. The three glimpses of the map encapsulate this change:

QUESTION
In what ways has Dora subverted male authority in her story? Think in terms of the extent to which patriarchalism extends beyond simply the men as characters.

CHECK THE BOOK
Carter once stated: 'The sense of limitless freedom that I, as a woman, sometimes feel *is* that of a new kind of being. Because I simply could not have existed, as I am, in any other preceding time or place. I am the pure product of an advanced, industrialised, post-imperialist country in decline' ('Notes from the Front Line', in *On Gender and Writing*, edited by Michelene Wandor, 1983).

- in the comedy act on Brighton Pier (Chapter 2, pp. 66–7)

- in Dora's stripping him of his Bottom costume on the Hollywood film set (Chapter 3, p. 157)

- in the London street outside Melchior's residence (Chapter 5, p. 196)

The map of the world is first seen in the patriotic fervour of singing and cheering at the end of his comedy act in Brighton. The colonial pink that covers many of the countries of the British Empire is splendid: 'brilliant'. In the second appearance, Dora takes off the clothes of the drunken George, feeling that she has 'exposed the British Empire'. She rolls him naked under a bush, commenting that she did not want 'our nation's shame out in the open for all to see' (Chapter 3, p. 157). She feels that 'It felt like the end of something', the 'it' being both music hall and empire. In its final appearance beneath the stained ex-army greatcoat, symbolising the decline of the British military power that formed and sustained an empire, the map is still visible, but its pink is faded. George, and all that he once stood for in terms of music hall and patriotic fervour for a British Empire, is reduced to begging in the street.

ILLUSION AND REALITY

The sections on **Carnival and carnivalesque** and **Magic realism** in **Approaches to *Wise Children*** carry over into this central theme. With a novel such as *Wise Children* it is difficult to separate some of the main features into self-contained compartments.

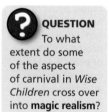

QUESTION
To what extent do some of the aspects of carnival in *Wise Children* cross over into **magic realism**?

Dora's questioning of the facts in her faulty memory or her reconstruction of past events often prompts the reader to ask whether the story is credible. In the context of the novel, as in a Shakespeare play, the willing suspension of disbelief is appropriate. The idea that a tale often bears distant or distorted resemblance to the facts extends beyond literature and drama. Our own experiences of hearing a tale retold, or of retelling a tale ourselves, reveal this. In a broader sense, for example the biblical tale of the Israelites' escape from Egypt and the destruction of their pursuers, it does not mean that what happened was not essentially true; it is simply that the telling of a wonderful event is built upon until the telling reveals the wonder. The same can be said to some extent of Dora's story, if we are to take it literally. Dora does frequently ask us to consider the credibility of what she is saying. For example, when she relates the events in Brighton (Chapter 2, pp. 68–9), the account is qualified on at least half a dozen occasions, until the prosaic reality of 'A quid less a tanner' brings the story back to the real world. Similarly, Peregrine's escape with the girls from the rejection of Melchior (Chapter 2, p. 72) is qualified by 'although I know it cannot be … true', a couple of alternative 'ors' and an admission that Dora is imagining a part of it.

CHECK THE BOOK
For another novel which uses the double perspective of adult/child narrator, see Charles Dickens's *Great Expectations* (1860–1).

In this world of the novel, however, some events are told with a blend of magic and realism that needs to be accepted in a different way. These events often have **carnivalesque** aspects, in which the normal order of reality is turned upside down. The fire at Lynde Court (pp. 100–7) has carnivalesque elements, but also, amid the realities of firemen and missing people, there is the overriding question: did things really happen like this? Peregrine's production of the new twins from his pockets is another example of conjuring in which the illusory sits alongside the reality (Chapter 5, p. 226).

Life imitating art, a reversal of the usual format, occurs frequently – notably in the Shakespeare re-enactments. The illusion that Shakespeare sometimes acknowledges himself in the text, in the same way that Dora does, involves disguises and mistaken identities taken to the extreme, for example the impersonation of Dora by the first wife of Genghis. Her appearance in the bushes, making Dora think for a moment that she is 'looking in a mirror' (Chapter 3, p. 155), stretches our suspension of disbelief.

In the romantic confusions on and off set in *The Dream* there is a doubly distorted sense of Shakespearian and Hollywood illusion merging with reality. Distorted already by exaggeration and excess, and a strange blend of American ceremony and English music hall, the whole scenario calls to mind Puck's statement: 'Lord, what fools these mortals be!' (*A Midsummer Night's Dream*, III.2.115). *A Midsummer Night's Dream* celebrates the dream world of illusion in the 'Land of Make-Believe' (Chapter 3, p. 120). However, just as in the play, the world of illusion is subject to the real world, and as the law of Athens restores order, so too in Hollywood some sense of normality returns. The main

CHECK THE BOOK
For a detailed synopsis of *A Midsummer Night's Dream*, as well as a comprehensive guide to the play's stage, film and television history, try *The Oxford Companion to Shakespeare*, edited by Michael Dobson and Stanley Wells (2001).

difference is that in Hollywood it is Tony's mother, Grandma Chance and Dora who bring about that order – a female reversal of the male-dominated fairy world of Oberon and the Duke of Athens.

The world of illusion and imagination must return to reality. While Peregrine might be content to see life as a carnival ('He was an illusionist, remember'), it is Dora who asserts the reality of the world with her exhortation to listen to the news. Peregrine's question 'What news?' (Chapter 5, p. 222) does not alter the fact that the carnival is over. The house is not brought down by carnivalesque behaviour, and a return to the reality below awaits them. Peregrine's spirit, however, is indefatigable – maybe the reason why he cannot remain long in one real place. The production of the twins is magical but real. The journey home, however fantastic the events beforehand, is definitely real (as underlined by the pram and the stop at the 'all-night Boots … for formula and bottles', and Nora and Dora putting their bags in the pram for safety). The singing and dancing in the street by the seventy-five-year-old grandmothers is put into place by the Rastafarian's call from the window of 41 Bard Road.

APPROACHES TO *WISE CHILDREN*

CARNIVAL AND CARNIVALESQUE

The Russian theorist Mikhail Bakhtin (1895–1975) is generally credited with popularising in the late twentieth century the terms 'carnival' and '**carnivalesque**' in relation to literature. In *Rabelais and His World* he traces through the grossly amusing writings of European folk culture and the unrestrained excesses of carnival.

Early European carnival was a far cry from the carnivals of today. It involved a complete inversion and thereby subversion of order. Authority of all kinds – political, ecclesiastical, social, moral – was turned on its head. In this topsy-turvy world all hierarchies and constraints were subverted. The blurring of the boundaries of class, culture, of male and female roles, and of real and false identities established an order of misrule and misbehaviour. Masks and cross-dressing, role play and coarse humour were integral features. It was a time of imitation and **parody**. Traditional hierarchical figures, notably kings and bishops, were mocked in performances, plays and processions. The boredom and rigidity of routine were replaced by laughter and a wild, joyful abandon. Carnival humour emphasised our common humanity and imperfection. Bodily functions that take us from cradle to grave emphasised vitality and the cycle of life. Man laughed at his inescapable, cyclical fate. The carnivalesque spirit evoked a sense of the creative/destructive force in nature and suggested a kind of regeneration.

Typical carnival events took place before Lent, on May Day, on Midsummer Day, during the harvest and on All Fools' Day, which was originally in December. The Twelfth Night revels after Christmas with the appointment of a Lord of Misrule over proceedings give some idea of the spirit of these occasions. In earlier medieval European practice, however, excesses in eating, drinking, sex and violence were often integral features. A representation of carnival can be seen in the painting *The Fight between Carnival and Lent* by Pieter Bruegel the Elder (1559).

Bakhtin extended this historical phenomenon into literature, art, philosophy – life itself. The idea of ridicule and the bringing down to earth of accepted standards and values occur in artistic creations. Thus carnivalisation or carnivalesque writing beyond the historical European context can be seen in literary creations as far apart as the **Menippean satire**, the novels of Dostoevsky, even the novels of Virginia Woolf, and the works of modern writers such as Angela Carter. In his work *The Spirit of Carnival: Magic Realism and the Grotesque* David K. Danow identifies some characteristics of carnivalesque literature:

- the blurring of boundaries between real and supernatural worlds

- acceptance of unacceptable ideas

- the possibility of magical elements in a real world

- the presentation of fiction as truth

CHECK THE BOOK

Bakhtin writes: 'The temporary suspension, both ideal and real, of hierarchical rank created during carnival time creates a special type of communication impossible in everyday life. This led to the creation of special forms of marketplace speech and gesture, frank and free, permitting no distance between those who came in contact with each other and liberating from norms of etiquette and decency imposed at other times' (in *Rabelais and His World*).

CHECK THE NET

For an image of Bruegel's *The Fight between Carnival and Lent*, visit **www.abcgallery. com**. The painting now hangs at the Kunsthistorisches Museum in Vienna.

CARNIVAL AND CARNIVALESQUE continued

CONTEXT

Bakhtin uses the term carnivalesque to analyse the work of the Russian novelist Fyodor Dostoevsky (*Rabelais and His World*). Other critics have used Bakhtin's ideas to explore writers such as Samuel Beckett (1906–89) and James Joyce (1882–1941) in a carnivalesque context.

Bakhtin also presents another dimension to the idea of carnivalesque in an alternative view of reality. Here it becomes a rebellious force that can destroy, change, liberate and renew. Modern demonstrations often employ carnivalesque images and techniques in this way.

In short, carnival refers to a specific, socio-historical phenomenon, while carnivalisation or the carnivalesque identifies the carnival spirit that can be found in **magic realism**.

MAGIC REALISM

Magic (or magical) realism is a term that is almost self-explanatory. It is a literary genre in which magical elements exist within a realistic context. Events, characters and settings are recognisably real, but incorporate magical elements. The term can also be used to describe paintings and films.

The term was first used in the 1920s in Europe. A German art critic, Franz Roh, used it to describe the work of post-Expressionist painters who were attempting to show reality in a different way. An Italian writer, Massimo Bontempelli, at the same time used the term to describe his own writing in his novel *Separations*. In the 1960s the term was used to describe the works of a number of Latin American novelists, notably Miguel Angel Asturias and Gabriel García Márquez. Márquez's *One Hundred Years of Solitude* (1967, translated into English in 1970) is considered by many critics to be the key modern magical realist writing.

Modern novelists whose works belong to some extent in this genre include Isabel Allende, Jorge Luis Borges, Peter Carey, Umberto Eco, John Fowles, Günter Grass, Peter Høeg, Ian McEwan, Salman Rushdie, Graham Swift and, of course, Angela Carter. There are others from other times and places, so it would be wrong to suggest that magic realism is solely a late twentieth-century movement. Indeed, magic realism is not a movement as such, perhaps only in some limited works a genre. It is more of a style or even an attitude to reality that features in some of the writings of novelists. Other earlier novels which could be considered in a magical realist manner include Franz Kafka's *Metamorphosis* (1916), Virginia Woolf's *Orlando* (1928) and, going even further back, Jonathan Swift's *Gulliver's Travels* (1726).

One problem with the term is that it is closely related to other genres or styles in literature, notably fantasy and science fiction, and in art surrealism; but magic realism may be said to have a number of characteristics which may appear in a novel. The essence of magic realism is that it exists in a recognisably real world, not an imaginary one. Its characters are real, not creations of the imagination. Incredible or illogical events are portrayed and accepted in the context of the **narrative**, though never explained fully. Frequently there is an abundance of rich sensory details. Often a number of **voices** provide different perspectives, notably concerning belief and disbelief. Legend, fairy tale or folklore enters the narrative. Time is often non-chronological and events in the present frequently mirror those in the past. The themes of magic realism are measured on the scale of the personal and human, rather than on the grander scale of the spiritual or cosmic. Finally, the moral stances of character, narrator and author are rarely totally clear; the boundaries between good and evil are not absolutely defined. The unacceptable (either in terms of credibility or morality) is accepted in the context of the story. The reader is drawn into the narrative (may be addressed directly) and is left uncertain as to the paradox of magical and realistic elements.

FEMINISM AND POST-FEMINISM

Feminism in its various forms (social, political, economic, moral, artistic) over the years has addressed the ways in which assumptions about women feature in aspects of society. In the broader sphere, as a social movement, feminism has attempted to promote the rights of women in societies that have been largely male orientated. It also has tried to show that male attitudes can accommodate a different role for women in society. Feminist writers, readers and critics attempt to show how literature can either promote or challenge male-dominated views and attitudes. The societies or cultures in which we live determine the way we read (or write) texts dealing with male and female identities. Feminist activists have promoted many views that deal with gender in the workplace, in marriage and sexual relationships, in social and domestic structures. In literature the themes that are addressed by a feminist approach include patriarchy, female stereotyping, the oppression of women and the treatment of women as objects.

CONTEXT

The boundaries of magic realism are not absolute; they can be blurred in places across a writer's work or within a story. Fantasy can be distinct from magic realism; J. R. R. Tolkien's *Lord of the Rings* (1954–5), for example, is not classed as magic realism.

CHECK THE BOOK

Susan Napier suggests that magical realism 'takes the supernatural for granted and spends more of its space exploring the game of human reactions': a view that could be used to describe *Wise Children* in many ways ('The Magic of Identity: Magic Realism in Modern Japanese Fiction', in *Magical Realism: Theory, History, Community*, edited by Lois Parkinson Zamora and Wendy B. Faris).

FEMINISM AND POST-FEMINISM continued

CONTEXT

Since the end of the 1960s, feminist theories about literature and language, together with feminist interpretations of text, have multiplied. Feminist criticism is now a significant field of literary study, to the point of being a subject for study in itself. Feminist criticism intends to redress the balance between the male-dominated aspects of society and interpretation of literature.

There are two approaches to challenging patriarchal attitudes in literature:

● to read into texts the gender imbalance

● to promote texts which present alternatives to male-dominated systems and viewpoints

The first is a critical approach to reading a text which may or may not be feminist per se. The second is to produce texts which challenge patriarchal views of women's role in society.

The history of feminism can be traced back to the eighteenth century, with Mary Wollstonecraft's *A Vindication of the Rights of Woman* appearing in 1792. Shortly after that, however, the term feminism was first used by Charles Fourier in 1837, this French social reformer already having argued the case for the rights of woman in a male-orientated society as early as 1808. Since then several writers have developed feminist thought. John Stuart Mill's *The Subjection of Women* appeared in 1869; Germaine Greer's *The Female Eunuch* was published one hundred years later in 1970. Significant modern texts are Betty Friedan's *The Feminine Mystique* (1963), Kate Millet's *Sexual Politics* (1970) and Naomi Wolf's *The Beauty Myth* (1991), while Germaine Greer revisits feminism in *The Whole Woman* (1999). For a brief survey of feminist thought, Susan Osborne's book *Feminism* (2001) is a useful starting point with simple explanations of the range of ideas in this movement.

CONTEXT

Second-wave feminism began in the 1960s as a politically motivated movement seeking equal rights. Some writers envisaged matriarchal communities, refuting, like Grandma Chance, war and violence, which were seen as male-dominated phenomena.

Post-feminism and the second- and third-wave movements that have followed it show how feminism has been refined in the light of changes in attitude over the years. A group of French theorists and literary critics in the latter decades of the twentieth century have extended the canon of feminist literature. Foremost among these are Hélène Cixous, Julia Kristeva and Luce Irigaray.

Angela Carter clearly contributes to modern feminist thought, though she did not use the term about her novels; in fact, she shunned the idea in the much quoted statement in 'Notes from the Front Line' (in *On Gender and Writing*, edited by Michelene Wandor, 1983): 'I believe that all myths are products of the human mind and reflect only aspects of material human practice. I'm in the demythologising business.' However, there is no doubt that Carter did contribute much to the feminist debate in novels, short stories and non-fictional texts and articles. In *Nothing Sacred: Selected Writings* (1982) she declared that 'in Japan I learned what it was to be a woman and became radicalised', and in 'Notes from the Front Line' added that she discovered a 'sense of heightened awareness of the society around me' and 'How that social fiction of my "femininity" was created'. Though she did once say that she 'didn't see the point of feminism' (*Independent on Sunday*, June 1991), she did also say in talking with John Mortimer that she wouldn't be the person she was 'if it weren't for the women's movement of the Sixties' (*Sunday Times*, 24 January 1982).

QUESTION
How does society tend to stereotype women in certain roles? Make a list of the roles that categorise stereotypical representations. What stereotypical roles for women are evident in *Wise Children*?

For an overview of the ways in which Carter explores the myths that surround women, Gina Wisker's *Angela Carter: A Beginner's Guide* (2003) provides the reader of *Wise Children* with sufficient background detail to the techniques and approaches she has used in earlier works. For more detailed analyses of the ways in which Carter explores attitudes about women, the essays in *Flesh and the Mirror: Essays on the Art of Angela Carter* (edited by Lorna Sage, 1994) are recommended. For enjoyable wider reading of Angela Carter, *The Passion of New Eve*, *The Magic Toyshop* and *Nights at the Circus* give some idea of the range of approaches Carter uses in her demythologising of gender stereotypes in novels. Carter also challenges male stereotypes of women in looking at fairy tales, folk tales, myths and legends, **Gothic** horror stories and the film industry.

Other writers whose works contribute to the modern debate include Margaret Atwood, Pat Barker in her early fiction, Judith Butler, Patricia Duncker, Sara Maitland, Emma Tennant, Fay Weldon and Jeanette Winterson. The Virago Press, on whose board Angela Carter sat, was founded in 1973 to promote women's writing and is still a major force in bringing women authors to public attention.

CHECK THE NET
To find out more about the lives and works of many of the modern writers mentioned in these Notes, and to read some insightful critical essays on their writings, go to **www.contemporary writers.com** and search the author index.

Feminist issues such as the exploration of patriarchalism, the role of fathers, relationships in marriage and in families, male-dominated

CHECK THE BOOK
Try Jeffrey Roessner's useful essay entitled 'Writing a History of Difference: Jeanette Winterson's *Sexing the Cherry* and Angela Carter's *Wise Children'* (*College Literature,* Winter 2002).

structures in other areas of society, the role of women as individuals, as well as the providers of alternative social structures, feature in *Wise Children* and offer many lines for critical exploration of the text.

NARRATIVE TECHNIQUE AND LANGUAGE

Postmodernism, post-feminism, carnival and the **carnivalesque** and **magic realism** feature behind or within the structure and approaches of *Wise Children.* The starting point for most examinations of the novel begins with the many things that *Wise Children* is. It is variously and simultaneously a romance, memoir, intended autobiography extending to family history, dramatic monologue, fairy tale, **parody, farce,** pantomime, carnival, satire, 'etc. etc. etc.', to quote Dora herself (Chapter 3, p. 158). The cast of thousands, as well as the twists and turns of several storylines, means that an equally lengthy **narrative** catalogue emerges – family relationships, love affairs, births, marriages (real and mock), deaths (real and mock), betrayals, loyalties, appearances and disappearances. This kaleidoscopic nature of style and plot, however, is unified by the narrator, Dora.

CONTEXT
On more than one occasion in the novel the voice of Grandma Chance is echoed in the voice of Dora the narrator, particularly in her tendency to merge the elevated with the profane. Such echoes raise questions about legitimacy in its broadest sense.

Dora's first-person narrative, a form that requires the reader to trust the tale rather than the teller, is acknowledged by her on a number of occasions to be unreliable and subject to question. She recognises too a less artistic concern at the start: 'Romantic illegitimacy, always a seller. It ought to copper-bottom the sales of my memoirs.' She goes on to suggest that there was nothing 'romantic' about their illegitimacy, but follows this with a more philosophical idea: 'But the urge has come upon me before I drop to seek out an answer to the question that always teased me, as if the answer were hidden, somewhere, behind a curtain: whence came we? Whither goeth we?' (Chapter 1, p. 11). This paragraph points to a prominent feature of narrative style and contrasting semantic fields. We have, on the one hand, the tone and vocabulary of the south London showgirl; and, on the other, the more refined, literate, philosophical, perhaps conscious, elevation of language.

Though it is monological in its narrator, other terms used by Bakhtin – polyphony and **dialogism** – apply in *Wise Children*. Dora allows for several **voices**, styles, viewpoints and sensibilities. This **polyphonic** quality occurs in narrative shifts that are quite obviously signalled, for example Gorgeous George's stage act (Chapter 2, pp. 64–6) or the extract from Irish's 'famous *Hollywood* stories' (Chapter 3, p. 119).

Nevertheless, *Wise Children* is Dora's story, her own account of her own life. Her English is frequently flawed, profane in both its narrow and broader sense. Colloquialisms appear often in her choice of word, a colourful simile, her freedom with grammar and sentence structures, movements between tenses often using the historical present. There are sudden shifts to address, question – even challenge – the reader; there are jokes, **allusions** and sudden shifts in time as a word or an image triggers a memory. These qualities produce a lively, honest voice, even if she does acknowledge: 'Can't keep a story going in a straight line, can I? Drunk in charge of a narrative' (Chapter 3, p. 158), and there is one moment at the end where she admits that her story resembles the sort of tale you might hear from some dubious old woman in the local pub:

> Well, you might have known what you were about to let yourself in for when you let Dora Chance in her ratty old fur … reeking of liquor, accost you in the Coach and Horses and let her tell you a tale.   (Chapter 5, p. 227)

At times, however, there are other voices and styles which work their way into the story. A consciously literate voice occasionally takes over. Is this perhaps the converse of what Carter claimed in *Expletives Deleted* (1992) to have happened to her, that the holy emerges amongst the profane? The surfacing of this literate voice may be down to another Irishman: not James Joyce, but Irish himself. His education programme has given Dora another voice. There is also the possibility that Carter, the author in charge of the narrator, may interpose her own parodies for satirical purposes. In the following example, it is up to us as readers to make our own minds up whether it is an unconscious awareness of Shakespeare's work, Dora debunking Melchior or Carter herself making fun of

CONTEXT

There is a public house, the Coach and Horses, on Clapham Road between Clapham and Brixton. An area off Railton Road, mentioned by Dora in *Wise Children*, has a number of streets named after literary figures including Shakespeare and Milton (although not quite Bard Road).

intertextuality. As they wait nervously in his dressing room, Dora describes how she and Nora have from time to time watched Melchior 'strut and fret his hour upon the stage' (Chapter 2, p. 71; taken from *Macbeth*, V.5.25). Whatever the purpose of this comment, it says as much about high culture as it does about Melchior in the role of Macbeth.

Shakespeare is everywhere in *Wise Children*. The play on words is frequently comic. Hamlet's 'To be, or not to be' becomes not a matter of life or death but a hotel address, '2b or not 2b', in the revue (Chapter 2, p. 90). More ludicrously, it becomes 'To butter or not to butter' in one of My Lady Margarine's television commercials (Chapter 1, p. 38). The play on words from the subtitle of *Twelfth Night* in Melchior's West End revue *What You Will* is parodied by Dora in the variety of punctuation possibilities that add innuendo to the original pun. The last one – '*What? You Will!?!*' (Chapter 5, p. 217) – is deliberately absurd.

The reference to Jane Austen at the start of Chapter 4 parodies not only her literary style, but may also be self-mockery at Dora's alphabetical instruction in English literature by Irish. This obvious intertextuality is complemented by several others echoing Milton ('Lo, how the mighty are fallen'), Graham Greene ('a burned-out case') and Dylan Thomas; and there are many other literary allusions, lines from songs, fairy-tale references, even the odd joke. Carter did admit to enjoying playing games with the reader in a text.

Dora's use of French may be accurate at times, but it can also smack of London: 'Some superannuated hoofers put on the avoirdupois like nobody's business' (Chapter 1, p. 6). It could be 'Del Boy' Trotter (from the TV comedy *Only Fools and Horses*) speaking in the descent from the correct 'superannuated' to the incorrect French and the pure cockney 'hoofers' and 'like nobody's business'. This frequent ability to descend from the elevated to the base, as Dora does here, places two voices in the same sentence at once. This use of **bathos** is generally comic and, true to carnival spirit, is used to bring down the traditional, the revered, the high.

CHECK THE BOOK

In *Angela Carter* (1998) Linden Peach examines how Angela Carter sees theatre as a subversive force and looks at how Carter uses the theatre, the carnivalesque and the masque as part of her blending of the artificial with the real.

CONTEXT

In Chapter 1 Dora admits as she and Nora 'slap' on the 'warpaint' that 'Nobody could say the Chance girls were going gently into that good night' (p. 6); this echoes the line 'Do not go gentle into that good night', the title and first line of a poem by Dylan Thomas.

Dora somehow is capable of aphorisms that are worthy of Oscar Wilde or Dorothy Parker. There are many examples in the same vein as 'Comedy is tragedy that happens to *other* people' (Chapter 5, p. 213). Again, this could be due to Irish's tuition, or perhaps it is Carter nudging her own voice into the text.

Another linguistic feature stems from the idea that carnival removes social barriers, reduces the high to the low and leads to a change in language. Look, for example, at Melchior as he pulls up his chair to watch his house burn down (Chapter 2, pp. 104–5). In his article 'Bakhtin's "carnivalesque" in 1950s British Comedy' Tom Sobshack argues that Bakhtin suggests in *Rabelais and His World* that

> the carnivalesque spirit, which turned everything topsy turvy, led eventually to a change in language. The difference between street language (the colloquial) and the language of the ruling class (the formal tongue of court and church) was narrowed when aristocrat and commoner mingled during the carnival.

In the final analysis, however, this story belongs to Dora, and in the course of her trawling through her memories and the 'archaeology' of her desk, she leaves us at the end with a legitimate work of art – a novel.

> **CONTEXT**
>
> Dora reveals her surprise at Nora's familiarity with Wilde, commenting: 'Fancy her knowing about Oscar Wilde', after Nora has wittily reworded a Wilde quip (Chapter 4, p. 192). By this stage in the novel, however, the girls', particularly Dora's, wit and literary prowess should no longer surprise us.

PART FOUR

CRITICAL HISTORY

CRITICAL RECEPTION

CONTEXT

Angela Carter died of cancer on 16 February 1992.

Wise Children was destined to be Angela Carter's final novel. There is little doubt that, in order to finish it, she put aside treatment of the cancer that would eventually lead to her death shortly after the book's publication. *Wise Children* was recognised as a marked change from her earlier, darker novels in its sense of fun and its dazzling array of characters and incident. Carole Angier's review in the *New Statesman* acknowledged these qualities along with the Shakespearian comic exuberance that permeates the novel (Carole Angier, 'Song and Dance', *New Statesman*, June 1992).

CHECK THE BOOK

Michael McKeon's *Theory of the Novel: A Historical Approach* (2000) is an excellent introduction to the history of the novel.

By the time of her death, Angela Carter was beginning to be seen as a major force in the modern novel. Salman Rushdie pointed out that 'here in Britain she somehow never quite had her due', but enjoyed a worldwide reputation. His view was that *Wise Children* was her finest work, commenting: 'The novel is written with her unique brand of deadly cheeriness.' Rushdie reiterated his belief that 'Angela Carter was a great writer' ('Angela Carter, 1940–92: A Very Good Wizard, a Very Dear Friend', *New York Times Book Review*, 8 March 1992). Reviews of *Wise Children* variously pointed out the novel's effortless movement 'from shock to coincidence … from suspense to thumpingly absurd resolution' (*Times Literary Supplement*), its 'celebration of wrong-sidedness' (*Independent on Sunday*), its creation of 'a complex philosophical work on the ambiguity of biological ties' (*Nation*) and its 'verbal exuberance, exotic figures of speech, filthy colloquialisms and more than a smattering of good jokes' (*The Guardian*).

Lorna Sage in her obituary entitled 'The Soaring Imagination' (*The Guardian*, 17 February 1992) felt that Carter had died 'at the height of her powers', and noted the 'boldness of her writing, her powers of enchantment and hilarity, her generous inventiveness'. Sage in a survey of British fiction lists a number of problems that militate against the success of writers in modern Britain.

These include the loss of a tradition, the idea that the 'novel is anybody's' and what she calls the 'attention-famine' (the problem of recognition for new writing). She leads up to the belief that '*Wise Children* deals with most of these issues with brilliance, maturity, hilarity, and inventiveness' ('The Tangled Roots of What We Write', *The Observer*, 2 May 1993).

John Bayley, whose obituary on Carter was seen by some in much the same light as Mark Antony's speech praising the dead Caesar, recognised the anti-patriarchal attitudes, the **Gothic** horror, the demythologising of familiar tales, the 'spirited arabesques and feats of descriptive imagination', but suggested that the political correctness and ideological position of the 'elusive category of the postmodernist novel' to which Carter finally returned enabled her to be 'good at having it both ways'. He went on to assert that 'Carter's achievement shows us how a certain style of good writing has politicized itself today, constituting itself as the literary branch of militant orthodoxy' ('Fighting for the Crown', *New York Times Book Review*, 23 April 1992).

> **CHECK THE BOOK**
> For examples of **postmodernist** writers read Truman Capote's *In Cold Blood* (1966) and Robert M. Pirsig's *Zen and the Art of Motorcycle Maintenance* (1974).

For a spirited refutation of John Bayley's view that Carter has 'made imagination itself into the obedient handmaid of ideology', Hermione Lee's essay '"A Room of One's Own, or a Bloody Chamber?": Angela Carter and Political Correctness' and Elaine Jordan's 'The Dangerous Edge' place Carter's blend of imagination and realism, her art and her feminism into a better perspective (both published in *Flesh and the Mirror: Essays on the Art of Angela Carter*, edited by Lorna Sage). Marina Warner sees Carter as a crucial figure in promoting feminist literature, not only in her own writings, but also in her support for other writers (such as Pat Barker, who in her early work was encouraged by Carter) and her work with Virago. Carter contributed to the establishment of a woman's voice in literature and was 'a crucial instrument in the forging of an identity for post-imperial, hypocritical, fossilised Britain' (Marina Warner, 'Obituary: Angela Carter', *The Independent*, 18 February 1992).

RECENT CRITICISM

It is only in relatively recent years that a body of critical works on Angela Carter has been established. The general approach has been to see a **postmodernist**, feminist writer who explored cultural, political and socio-historical issues in fiction and non-fiction texts. The problem of labels, be they postmodern, feminist, magical realist, **carnivalesque** or whatever, needs to be addressed when you are dealing with criticism. A writer or a critic may display aspects of these approaches to a greater or a lesser extent. The labels are only useful in so far as they guide your reading of a text.

Lorna Sage is a good starting point for your readings of critical works. She has produced two important critical works on Carter: *Angela Carter* (1994) and *Flesh and the Mirror: Essays on the Art of Angela Carter* (1994). The latter is a collection of essays edited by Sage, covering Carter's novels, short stories and non-fiction from a variety of angles and providing a comprehensive survey of her works, as well as detailed commentary on *Wise Children*.

 CHECK THE NET
A senior lecturer at the University of Wales, Swansea, Sarah Gamble is a specialist in contemporary women's fiction who has written several useful texts and articles, and has her own website: go to www.swan.ac.uk and type 'Sarah Gamble's home page' into the search engine.

One of the main critical authorities is Sarah Gamble. In *Angela Carter: A Literary Life* (2005) she takes the reader through the maze of titles ascribed to Carter from the magical realist fairy godmother to Carter's own view of herself as a demythologiser and a materialist. Carter is placed in a cultural, social, political and theoretical context and the themes that appear in her work such as feminism, class, politics and English identity are developed through analyses of her novels, short stories and other writings. In *The Fiction of Angela Carter: A Reader's Guide to Essential Criticism* (2001) Gamble explores critical responses to Carter with attention to the **Gothic**, fairy-tale and science-fiction genres. The postmodern influence on her subversive approaches to gender and identity is also addressed. In *Angela Carter: Writing from the Front Line* (1997) Gamble looks at how Carter's work was influenced by her desire to subvert in terms of society, politics, gender, morality, history and the way that books come to be written. She comments that Carter 'sustains a tension between the time of history and the timelessness of myth as she undermines the metaphysical foundations of gender history'.

Humour in its various forms (satirical, **ironic, parodic,** pantomimic, carnivalesque) is an essential part of the subversion. Its roots may lie with Bakhtin: 'Laughter purifies from dogmatism, from the intolerant and the petrified; it liberates from fanaticism and pedantry, from fear and intimidation, from didacticism, naïveté and illusion, from the single meaning, the single level, from sentimentality' (Mikhail Bakhtin, *Rabelais and His World*). However, many suggest that Carter's humour owes more to Shakespeare and his comic world. Both lines of thought are worth exploring in your reading. Susan Rubin Suleiman says that 'the mood of her last published novel, *Wise Children*, is magnificently comic, with a self-consciously Shakespearian cast' ('The Fate of the Surrealist Imagination in the Society of the Spectacle', in *Flesh and the Mirror: Essays on the Art of Angela Carter*, edited by Sage).

Linden Peach in his book *Angela Carter* (1997) looks at how 'her novels deconstruct the processes that produce social structures and shared meaning', particularly in her demythologising of the mother figure and constructed views of woman in society. Peach examines Carter's subversion of the old myths and emphasises her control of language in the process of transgressing, her breaking of the rules in order to gain autonomy. Close readings of her texts provide ideas about themes, ideas, image and language. The magical realist and fantastic elements are shown to be relevant to the reality of people's lives in Carter's approach to philosophy, culture and literature. Peach notes 'the connection between *Wise Children* and the emergence of autobiography and oral history as important feminist narrative forms in the 1970s'.

Angela Carter: Contemporary Critical Essays, edited by Alison Easton (New Casebooks, 2004), provides a variety of essays showing feminist theoretical approaches. It includes the essay 'Seriously Funny: *Wise Children*' by Kate Webb, which also appears in the *Flesh and the Mirror* collection, edited by Sage.

In *Wise Children*'s portrayal of men and patriarchal attitudes in the family, as well as in the theatre and in Hollywood, Carter offers alternatives values and structures, and this contributes to the feminist debate. Dora and Nora subvert traditional, stereotypical assumptions about gender. Michael Hardin comments that they

CHECK THE FILM

Michael Hoffman's 1999 Hollywood version of *A Midsummer Night's Dream* sets the play in Tuscany in the late nineteenth century, and stars Kevin Kline as Bottom and Michelle Pfeiffer as Titania.

are able to 'escape patriarchal constraints by confusing their public external identities at the same time that they affirm and define their personal and individual identities' ('The Other Other: Self-Definition Outside Patriarchal Institutions in Angela Carter's *Wise Children*', in *Review of Contemporary Fiction*, Volume 14, 1994). Gender roles in the real world, in the theatre and in that blurring of the boundaries between reality and illusion occur in a variety of ways in *Wise Children*. This enables Carter to extend the debate surrounding gender and performance which is explored in her other novels, notably *Nights at the Circus* (1984). This is the subject of a number of essays in *The Infernal Desires of Angela Carter: Fiction, Femininity, Feminism*, edited by Malcolm Bradbury and Trev Lynn Broughton (1997).

Carter's position as a magical realist and as an artist committed to social and cultural criticism is discussed at some length by Linden Peach. The reconciling of the real world and Carter's carnivalesque settings is one of the debates you need to enter. It is one of the pleasures of reading closely a work which accommodates such disparate, contradictory elements. Carter can recreate the seafront at Brighton, the streets of London, the shabbiness of post-war, run-down theatres with details of time and place, but can also place into these contexts a strange world of magic that is at once illusory and real. Laura Mulvey points out that 'Transformations and metamorphoses recur so frequently in Angela Carter's writing that her books seem to be pervaded by this magic cinematic attribute even when the cinema itself is not present on the page.' Peregrine's interest in butterflies, she says, is 'emblematic of metamorphosis' ('Cinema Magic and the Old Monsters: Angela Carter's Cinema', in *Flesh and the Mirror*). Linden Peach suggests that Carter uses alienating techniques like the fantastic and the magical, while remaining always socially committed. In *Come Unto These Yellow Sands* Carter asserts: 'for me, a narrative is an argument stated in fictional terms' (1985).

David K. Danow in *The Spirit of Carnival: Magical Realism and the Grotesque* (1995) examines the way in which magic realism can operate in a text such as *Wise Children*:

> Magical realism manages to present a view of life that exudes a sense of energy and vitality in a world that promises not only

CHECK THE NET
'It was her particular feat to be able to marry the high with the low, the erudite with the bawdy. Her glee in mingling philosophy and the circus, realism and fantasy, knowledge and kitchen gossip, is positively impish. In her last novel, *Wise Children*, the Chance sisters high-kick their way through Shakespeare – irreverent, like Carter, to the last.' To read the full article, 'Flight Entertainment', by Lisa Appignanesi go to **www.guardian. co.uk** and search for Lisa Appignanesi and Angela Carter.

joy, but a fair share of misery as well. In effect, the reader is rewarded with a perspective on the world that still includes much that elsewhere has been lost, where 'possible' is instantly transformed into probable as we are transported from the domain of the real by the similarly unchartered stratagems of the artistic imagination.

Aidan Day talks of the 'variety and multiplicity of life on the streets of her beloved London' in the novels, yet relates this not only to Carter's social belief in 'an alternative cultural model of reciprocity, tolerance and equality', but also to her ability to incorporate the fantastical into these real worlds and real views about society. Celestine Deleyto believes that *Wise Children* is not a historical novel, because Dora adopts a stance external to patriarchal history. The family names identify 'that which history is not – Chance, then, not causality, governs the development of the narrative' ('We are no Angels: Woman Versus History in Angela Carter's *Wise Children*', in *In Telling Histories: Narrativizing History, Historicizing Literature*, edited by Susan Onega).

CHECK THE BOOK

Aidan Day's *Angela Carter: The Rational Glass* (1998), is a chronological examination of Carter's fiction with clear accounts of influences and theoretical interpretations.

PART FIVE

BACKGROUND

ANGELA CARTER

Angela Carter was born Angela Stalker in Eastbourne, Sussex, in 1940. Her father was a journalist from Scotland; her mother was from a mining community in South Yorkshire. During the Second World War Angela moved north to Yorkshire to live with her maternal grandmother, who was working class and down to earth, a domineering matriarchal figure and a feminist. These formative years away from the family home under the influence of her grandmother clearly informed Carter's attitudes and her later writings. Returning to the family home in London after the war, Angela suffered for a time from anorexia. The absence of mother figures in Carter's fiction has never been fully explained, though grandmother figures are prominent, notably in *Wise Children*.

Angela Carter's interest in film and the glamour of Hollywood began with her visits to the cinema with her father. The United States, too, held a fascination, more so in the 1950s since it represented a world far away from the austerity of post-war Britain. This decade saw the emergence of rock and roll, the anti-hero and a rebelliousness of spirit among the young. The angry young men and the more violent Teddy boys in colourful Edwardian 'gear' added to a vibrant youth culture that contradicted traditional values. Carter's desire to shock, in her fiction as well as on occasions in real life, possibly has its roots in this era.

Carter married at the age of twenty before she began her English studies, specialising in medieval literature, at Bristol University. She stayed on in Bristol after graduating in 1965. Three early novels, *Shadow Dance* (1966), *Several Perceptions* (1968) and *Love* (1971), comprise what is often referred to as her Bristol trilogy. *Shadow Dance* introduces the theme of sexual identity which would feature prominently throughout her writing career. This theme was developed in her second novel *The Magic Toyshop* (1967), in which

CONTEXT

The expression 'angry young man' was used to refer to a member of a group of socially conscious writers in the 1950s, including the playwright John Osborne. In Osborne's play *Look Back in Anger* (first performed in 1956, and published in 1957) the anti-hero Jimmy Porter articulated the characteristic views of the angry young man.

a young girl's growth through adolescence in her uncle's house is charted through sexual fantasy. Recognition for Carter came with the awarding of the John Llewellyn Rhys Prize for *The Magic Toyshop* in 1967, and the Somerset Maugham Award for *Several Perceptions* in 1969.

Separating from her husband in 1969, Carter spent a couple of years in Japan. Her return to England in 1972 signalled a prolific period of significant writing. *The Infernal Desire Machines of Dr Hoffman* (1972) tells the story of the eponymous evil doctor, who attempts to free mankind by destroying the principle of reality. The transmission of erotic images through the mirrors of the world enable people to follow their desires rather than the dictates of society. Her journalistic work at this time owes much to her stay in Japan, which enabled her to see English culture and values from an outside perspective. In *The Passion of New Eve* (1977) a feminist surgeon changes a chauvinistic, sexist male into a female, and starts to programme him/her into a female identity. Before the programme is complete he/she escapes but is left to resolve the problem of a male mind trapped in a female body. *The Sadeian Woman* (1979) is, as its subtitle tells us, an exercise in cultural history. This non-fiction work challenges accepted views of sexuality and explores the sadistic and masochistic aspects of human relationships and suffering.

Two collections of short stories, *Fireworks: Nine Profane Pieces* (1974) and *The Bloody Chamber and Other Stories* (1979), were written during this period. *Fireworks* draws from her experiences of Japanese culture with its ceremonial formality and its brooding erotic nature. The other stories introduce the dark world of fable, which will figure significantly in future works. Another figure that appears at this point is the monstrous woman with unsated appetites, who will reappear in *The Bloody Chamber*. In this collection, with its opening long short story and nine shorter ones, **Gothic** rewritings of folklore and fairy tale bring strange metamorphoses and sinister reversals. Dark imagery and themes of sexual desires and dangers combine to create a rich blend that offers the finest in Carter's fiction, and is possibly the best comprehensive introduction to her work.

> **CONTEXT**
>
> In her introduction to *The Virago Book of Fairy Tales* Carter says that 'fairy tales, folk tales, stories from the oral tradition, are all of them the most vital connection we have with the imaginations of ordinary men and women whose labour created our world' (1990).

During this period in the seventies Carter remarried and began a series of engagements in teaching creative writing, first of all at Sheffield University from 1976 to 1978. Further teaching posts in the next decade in America (Brown University, Rhode Island, 1980–1), in Australia (University of Adelaide, 1984) and in England (University of East Anglia, 1984–7) enhanced her reputation as an inspiring teacher of writing.

In 1984 the cinematographic qualities of Carter's prose were recognised in two successful adaptations on screen. *The Company of Wolves*, directed by Neil Jordan and using material from the collection *The Bloody Chamber*, appeared as a film. In 1987 Granada TV produced a version of *The Magic Toyshop*, directed by David Wheatley.

 CHECK THE BOOK

According to Lorna Sage: 'Angela Carter's life ... is the story of someone walking a tightrope. It's all happening "on the edge" in no-man's land, among the debris of past convictions. By the end, her life fitted her more or less like a glove, but that's because she'd put it together by trial and error, bricolage, all in the (conventionally) wrong order. Her genius and estrangement came out of a thin-skinned extremity of response to the circumstances of her life and to the sign of the times' ('Death of the Author', *Granta: Biography*, 41, Autumn 1992; published in an expanded form in Sage's 1994 work *Angela Carter*).

Carter's last two major novels, *Nights at the Circus* (1985) and *Wise Children* (1991), have much in common. Both explore the non-legitimate side of theatre, the former circus performance, the latter pantomime, music hall and Hollywood. Fevvers and Dora Chance take firm control of their stories/histories as narrators conscious of their careers on the other side of the tracks but determined to assert their identities. Both novels have **carnivalesque** features of plot, **narrative**, language, imagery, characterisation and attitude. In *Nights at the Circus* Fevvers, the winged lady, tells her story from brothel to travelling circus, escaping from patriarchal constraints into song and spectacle. Picaresque and carnivalesque, the novel is an exuberant assertion of identity.

Sadly *Wise Children* was to be Carter's last novel. Her death only a few months after its publication, on 16 February 1992, came cruelly at the height of her powers and increasing stature and popularity. *Wise Children* encapsulates much of Carter's own personality in its power to enchant and to amuse, in its seriousness and its ribald humour, in its exploration of the illusions and realities that are close to us all. Perhaps, above all, it is its joyful and wilful celebration of life ('What a joy it is to dance and sing!') that defiantly, joyfully and, ultimately, **ironically** rings out in her last words of fiction.

HISTORICAL BACKGROUND

The lives of Dora and Nora span the twentieth century, while the Hazard family history goes back into the later decades of the nineteenth century. Though *Wise Children* weaves its way in and out of history, selectively omitting or glossing over major world events such as the two world wars, the Depression years and the political events in post-war Britain, there are significant historical points of reference that aid our understanding of the context of the novel and of Angela Carter's career. Rather than going through the historical background in chronological order, it seems appropriate for a novel such as *Wise Children* to identify these strands of history and deal with them separately. The strands are:

- the British Empire

- changes in Britain and London

- the world of entertainment

THE BRITISH EMPIRE

The period from the mid 1860s to the first decades of the twentieth century saw the British Empire cover a quarter of the globe and govern approximately one fifth of the world's peoples. From Canada, Central and South America, across Africa, in India and other territories in Asia, down to Australia and New Zealand, with several smaller, strategic islands in between, the British Empire quite literally straddled the globe. Besides governing these territories, British culture and religion were also introduced to several disparate countries in the belief that Britain was, as Lord Curzon, Viceroy of India, put it, 'the greatest force for good the world has seen'. Patriotic pride and fervour were reinforced in many ways: education, the establishment of Empire Day in 1902, the royal parades with exotic 'rulers' in attendance, colonial pavilions and imperial monuments.

However, the decline of empire was almost inevitable. Powers with greater resources – Germany, Russia and the United States – were becoming increasingly influential in world affairs. A democratising spirit in the mid twentieth century meant that ideas of

> **CONTEXT**
>
> Appropriately, a music hall song of the time captures the exaggerated sense of national pride: 'We are getting it by degrees, we are getting it by degrees, / We get a bit here, we get a bit there, / The Union Jack is everywhere, / And now and then we give it a gentle squeeze, / We haven't got the whole world yet – but we're getting it by degrees' (quoted in *The Navy and Defence* by E. Chatfield, 1942).

independence and autonomy were challenging the right of one nation to rule others' affairs. This inevitable decline of imperial power was witnessed by many in the early part of the twentieth century. Simon Schama says: 'Even the most swollen-headed imperialist was not such a fool as to need reminding by the likes of Kipling that all this too, some day, would pass' (*A History of Britain: The Fate of Empire*, Volume 3, 2002). The process of decline can be traced across the century from Egypt's semi-autonomy and Ireland's semi-independence in 1921–2, through India's eventual independence from British rule in 1947, which was followed in the fifties and sixties by several other nations gaining independence. Many of these nations became a part of the British Commonwealth, which eventually became simply the Commonwealth, a loose organisation of independent countries. Economic and political factors had brought a virtual end to what had been half a century previously a massive empire.

CHANGES IN BRITAIN AND LONDON

Late nineteenth-century Britain, the Victorian era, was to some extent dominated by the expansion of the British Empire and the prevailing attitude that colonialism was generally good for everyone. The Industrial Revolution had created a new power base, as the aristocracy had to bow to the wealth of newly rich industrialists and businessmen. The growth of cities was another consequence of the Industrial Revolution. Many cities, London included, had distinct social demographic zones, the poor living in cramped conditions in inner cities, the better-off in suburban areas. This was made possible by improved rail transport, which also led to the development of seaside resorts. Resorts such as Blackpool and Brighton catered for increasing numbers of workers for whom they introduced the amusement pier. The nineteenth century is frequently associated with the work ethic, family values, religious observation and faith in the institutions, religious and political. Families were patriarchal and supported the ideas of hard work, respect, obedience and conformity. However, increased educational opportunities following the Education Act of 1870 meant that many women were finding roles outside the traditional expectations.

CHECK THE NET

For a brief, clear account of the suffragette movement and, more generally, the role of women in twentieth-century Britain, visit **www.history learningsite.co.uk**

The first defining event of the twentieth century was the First World War (1914–18), a watershed in many ways. Britain was under threat, possibly of invasion from German forces, especially in terms of civilian life in London and the south. Conscription meant that thousands of young men fought in France, where the death toll was huge. By the end of the war terrible losses meant that many villages and towns were virtually emptied of young men. During the war, women were called upon to work in factories and in jobs traditionally done by men. The post-war years were characterised by a return to pre-war industrial unrest as more became aware of the inequalities of the old system that men had fought to protect. The promise by the prime minister, David Lloyd George, of a 'land fit for heroes' had not materialised. Unemployment was high, and poverty and deprivation added to the country's problems. Women too had gained an impetus through the suffragette movement that had begun in the pre-war years. The right of women to vote came in two almost begrudging stages – women over thirty were allowed to vote in 1918, while the right was extended to women over twenty-one in 1928.

The Wall Street Crash of 1929 led to the Depression, a period of economic and industrial decline that only ended with rearmament plans in the late 1930s for what was to be the Second World War. Again there was a sense of menace as invasion seemed a likelihood. Many English cities, notably London and Coventry, came under severe attack during the war in the Blitz. In the face of this threat many children were evacuated to safer rural areas in Wales and the north of England, a social phenomenon that carried many repercussions in later years.

The years following the Second World War, though troubled by the Suez Crisis in 1956, were considered to be a generally pleasant and increasingly affluent time with low unemployment and a higher standard of living. However, new immigrants, invited to Britain from the former colonies in the West Indies, experienced problems from some sectors of society unwilling to accept immigration policies. The late 1950s saw race riots in Notting Hill and in Nottingham. The sixties were years of further affluence and a sense of liberation after the austerity of the immediate post-war years.

CHECK THE BOOK

'And by their hundreds of thousands little boys and girls and not so little boys and girls – some in their best flannel short trousers; some, from the terraced streets of Stepney and Salford and Swansea, a bit snottier and scruffier and, as horrified evacuation hosts discovered, lousier – lined up at railway and bus stations on their way to the unthreatened countryside' (Simon Schama, *A History of Britain: The Fate of Empire*, Volume 3, 2002).

CHECK THE BOOK

For some idea of how Brixton in particular was affected by social movements and immigration in the twentieth century, Jerry White's *London in the Twentieth Century: A City and Its People* (2001) provides background to the worlds that Dora and Nora, as well as Angela Carter herself, were familiar with.

A youth culture had begun in the fifties with the advent of rock and roll music and this continued in the sixties with the emergence of the Beatles and the Rolling Stones. Fashion gained a new importance and the idea of 'swinging' England took hold.

However, the seventies became a period of discontent and economic decline that culminated in what was known as the Winter of Discontent in 1978 and the downfall of the Labour government. Starting in 1979 and running through the eighties, Margaret Thatcher brought in a series of social and political changes that included privatisation of nationalised industries, private ownership of council houses and private health care. There were serious riots in many areas, notably Brixton and Toxteth, Liverpool; and relationships between police and young people were difficult. Further problems were caused in 1990 with the poll tax demonstrations, culminating in the downfall of the Conservative government. The Conservative government retained control after the dismissal of Margaret Thatcher as leader, but it was Tony Blair who saw out the final three years of the century as prime minister under the banner of New Labour.

THE WORLD OF ENTERTAINMENT

CONTEXT

Henry Irving (1838–1905) was the first English actor to receive a knighthood. He made his London acting debut in 1866 at the St James's Theatre; in 1871 he transferred to the Lyceum, and earned the reputation as the greatest English actor of his time. His theatrical partnership with actress Ellen Terry began in 1878, and lasted until 1902.

The difference between legitimate theatre with its idea of high culture and non-legitimate theatre with its low culture association became apparent in the mid nineteenth century. Folk culture had always existed in songs and entertainments at fairs. In the eighteenth century legitimate drama in London had been virtually replaced by the new playhouses, which offered music, song, dance and juggling. Generally theatre and opera were regarded as middle- and upper-class interests.

The nineteenth century saw the emergence of the actor-managers, who often chose plays not so much for their quality but for the opportunity provided by the nature of the lead role. As a result, Shakespeare with opportunities to play Lear, Macbeth, Othello and Hamlet became popular. One of the great actor-managers was Henry Irving at the Lyceum. By the 1850s a distinct popular style began to emerge in the music halls with popular, contemporary, catchy songs, comedians and speciality acts of all types including dancers, acrobats, jugglers, animal acts and many one-off acts such as fire-eating or stilt-walking. Over fifty music halls and the so-called 'theatres of variety' were to be found in London in 1912. Music hall lasted from this period to the 1940s, though from about 1912 it was in decline, faced with twentieth-century developments in film and radio. There were over three hundred film licences granted in London at this time. By the end of the First World War an estimated three thousand cinemas had appeared across the country, and this figure had almost doubled by 1939. In the declining years of music hall some dancers turned to nude revues and strip shows (as Dora and Nora do in *Wise Children*), which grew in popularity in the 1950s.

The film industry grew rapidly in the United States with Thomas Edison taking out motion-picture patents in New Jersey in the first decade of the century. Hollywood was established as a major film centre at about the same time, partly to escape the patent laws and partly because of the brighter natural light of the sunnier West Coast. Many famous film studios developed, including Metro-Goldwyn-Mayer, Paramount, RKO, Twentieth Century Fox and Warner Brothers. In the period from 1927 (when sound films replaced the earlier silent movies) to about 1950 the growth in films gave birth to the 'Golden Age of Hollywood'. Actors from all over the world came to Hollywood. The film industry suffered a decline in the sixties and seventies, with many cinemas across Britain closing down. Television had done for the film industry what it, in turn, had done for the music halls. However, the film industry survived and has enjoyed a revival in recent years.

CHECK THE BOOK

For entertaining reading concerning the music hall and the travelling Pierrot shows, J. B. Priestley's novels *The Good Companions* (1965) and *Lost Empires* (1965) are recommended. John Osborne's play *The Entertainer* (published in 1957) provides a further insight into the lives of music hall comedians.

CHECK THE BOOK

Dreams for Sale: Popular Culture in the Twentieth Century, edited by Richard Maltby (1989), gives informative text and valuable visual materials, not only for music hall and Hollywood, but also for the general spirit of the times in terms of traditional culture and market forces across the twentieth century.

World events	Angela Carter's life	Literary events
		1850 Beginnings of music hall
1860–1914 British Empire		
		1912 Cinema introduced
1914–18 First World War		
		1927 First talking film, *The Jazz Singer*
1928 Women in UK gain equal voting rights		
1929 Wall Street Crash		1929 First film musical, *Broadway Melody*
1930s The Depression years		
1939–45 Second World War		
1940 Battle of Britain and start of the Blitz	1940 Born in Eastbourne	1940 Graham Greene, *The Power and the Glory*
		1941 Suicide of Virginia Woolf
1944 D-Day landings		1944 T. S. Eliot, *Four Quartets*
		1945 George Orwell, *Animal Farm*
1948 Assassination of Gandhi		
		1949 George Orwell, *Nineteen Eighty-Four*
1951 Festival of Britain		1951 Anthony Powell, first novel in series *A Dance to the Music of Time*
1953 Coronation of Queen Elizabeth II		1953 L. P. Hartley, *The Go-Between*

World events	Angela Carter's life	Literary events
1954 End of food rationing		**1954** William Golding, *Lord of the Flies*; Kingsley Amis, *Lucky Jim*; J. R. R. Tolkien, *The Fellowship of the Ring*; Dylan Thomas, *Under Milk Wood*
		1955 Samuel Beckett, *Waiting for Godot*; Philip Larkin, *The Less Deceived*
		1956 John Osborne, *Look Back in Anger*
1957 Harold Macmillan becomes prime minister; he makes his 'our people have never had it so good' speech		**1957** John Osborne, *The Entertainer*
		1958 Graham Greene, *Our Man in Havana*
	1959 Works on *Croydon Advertiser*	
1960 Macmillan makes his 'wind of change' speech in South Africa	**1960** Marries Paul Carter	**1960** Robert Bolt, *A Man for All Seasons*; Penguin Books acquitted in obscenity trial for publication of *Lady Chatterley's Lover*
1960s Several nations in former British Empire gain independence		**1961** Muriel Spark, *The Prime of Miss Jean Brodie*; *Private Eye* magazine founded; Royal Shakespeare Company founded
1962 Cuban missile crisis	**1962–5** Reads English at Bristol University	**1962** Anthony Burgess, *A Clockwork Orange*
1963 Assassination of President John F. Kennedy		

World events	Angela Carter's life	Literary events
		1964 Philip Larkin, *The Whitsun Weddings*
		1965 Sylvia Plath, *Ariel*
	1966 Begins reviews for *New Society* and *The Guardian*; first novel, *Shadow Dance*, published	1966 John Fowles, *The Magus*; Jean Rhys, *Wide Sargasso Sea*
1967 The Beatles, *Sergeant Pepper's Lonely Hearts Club Band*	1967 *The Magic Toyshop*; wins John Llewellyn Rhys Prize	1967 Tom Stoppard, *Rosencrantz and Guildenstern Are Dead*; Gabriel García Márquez, *One Hundred Years of Solitude* (translated into English 1970)
1968 Assassinations of Robert Kennedy and Martin Luther King	1968 *Several Perceptions*	
1969 Neil Armstrong becomes first man on the moon; riots in Northern Ireland; student protests in London	1969 *Heroes and Villains*; wins Somerset Maugham Award for *Several Perceptions*; separates from husband	1969 John Fowles, *The French Lieutenant's Woman*; Booker Prize initiated
	1970 *The Donkey Prince*	1970 Germaine Greer, *The Female Eunuch*
	1970–2 Lives in Japan	
1971 Women's Liberation march in London	1971 *Love*	
1972 Miners' strike	1972 Returns from Japan; divorces Paul Carter; *The Infernal Desire Machines of Dr Hoffman*	
1974 Miners' strike		
1975 Margaret Thatcher becomes leader of Conservative Party		1975 Malcolm Bradbury, *The History Man*; Jorge Luis Borges, *The Book of Sand*

World events	Angela Carter's life	Literary events
	1976–8 Arts Council Fellow at Sheffield University	
1977 Punk rock	1977 *The Passion of New Eve*; lives in South London with Mark Pearce; member of Virago Press advisory board	
1978 First test-tube baby		1978 Ian McEwan, *The Cement Garden*
1979 Margaret Thatcher becomes prime minister	1979 *The Bloody Chamber and Other Stories*; *The Sadeian Woman: An Exercise in Cultural History*; *Martin Leman's Comic and Curious Cats*	
1980 Riots in Bristol	1980 *The Music People*	1980 Umberto Eco, *The Name of the Rose*; William Golding, *Rites of Passage*
	1980–1 Visiting professor of creative writing at Brown University, Rhode Island	
1981 Riots in Liverpool, Manchester and Brixton; CND rally at Greenham Common		1981 Salman Rushdie, *Midnight's Children*
1982 Falklands War	1982 *Moonshadow*	1982 Caryl Churchill, *Top Girls*; Alice Walker, *The Color Purple*
	1983 Birth of son Alexander Pearce	1983 Grace Nichols, *I is a Long-Memoried Woman*

World events	Angela Carter's life	Literary events
1984 Violent clashes between miners and police	**1984** Writer in residence at University of Adelaide, South Australia; *Nights at the Circus*; film of *The Company of Wolves*	**1984** Julian Barnes, *Flaubert's Parrot*; Ted Hughes appointed Poet Laureate
	1984–7 Part-time teacher at University of East Anglia	
1985 Riots in Birmingham and London	**1985** *Black Venus* anthology; wins James Tait Memorial Prize for *Nights at the Circus*; teaches in Austin, Texas	**1985** Jeanette Winterson, *Oranges Are Not the Only Fruit*; Margaret Atwood, *The Handmaid's Tale*; Gabriel García Márquez, *Love in the Time of Cholera* (translated into English 1988)
	1986 Teaches in Iowa City, Iowa	
	1987 Television film of *The Magic Toyshop*	**1987** Ian McEwan, *The Child in Time*; Toni Morrison, *Beloved*
	1988 Teaches in Albany, New York State	**1988** Salman Rushdie, *The Satanic Verses*
1989 Fall of Berlin Wall		**1989** Kazuo Ishiguro, *The Remains of the Day*; Martin Amis, *London Fields*
1990 Violent demonstrations against poll tax in London; Mrs Thatcher resigns; John Major becomes prime minister		**1990** Hanif Kureishi, *The Buddha of Suburbia*
1991 Gulf War	**1991** *Wise Children*	**1991** Ben Okri, *The Famished Road*
	1992 Dies 16 February	

OTHER WORKS BY ANGELA CARTER

NOVELS

Shadow Dance (also published under the title *Honeybuzzard*), 1966

The Magic Toyshop, 1967

Several Perceptions, 1968

Heroes and Villains, 1969

Love, 1971

The Infernal Desire Machines of Dr Hoffman, 1972

The Passion of New Eve, 1977

Nights at the Circus, 1984

Wise Children, 1991

CHILDREN'S STORIES

Miss Z, the Dark Young Lady, 1970

The Donkey Prince, 1970

Martin Leman's Comic and Curious Cats, 1979

The Music People (with Leslie Carter), 1980

Moonshadow, 1982

Sea-Cat and Dragon King, 2000

COLLECTIONS

Fireworks: Nine Profane Pieces, 1974

The Bloody Chamber and Other Stories, 1979

FURTHER READING

Come Unto These Yellow Sands: Four Radio Plays, 1985

Black Venus (also published under the title *Saints and Strangers*), 1985

Artificial Fire, 1988

American Ghosts and Old World Wonders, 1993

Burning Your Boats: Collected Short Stories, 1995

The Curious Room: Collected Dramatic Works, 1996

Shaking a Leg: Collected Journalism and Writings, 1997

NON-FICTION
The Sadeian Woman: An Exercise in Cultural History, 1979

Nothing Sacred: Selected Writings, 1982

Images of Frida Kahlo, 1989

Expletives Deleted: Selected Writings, 1992

CRITICISM AND BACKGROUND READING

Flora Alexander, *Contemporary Women Novelists*, Arnold, 1989
Deals with Carter's earlier works *The Magic Toyshop, The Bloody Chamber and Other Stories* and *Nights at the Circus*

Kenneth Anger, *Hollywood Babylon*, Straight Arrow Books, 1975
A fascinating background to Hollywood and its stars

Isobel Armstrong (ed.), *New Feminist Discourses: Critical Essays on Theories and Texts*, Routledge, 1992
An essay by Elaine Jordan summarises criticism of Carter's work

Mikhail Bakhtin, *Rabelais and His World*, translated by Hélène Iswolsky, Indiana University Press, 1984
The source for much of the ideas of carnival and its terminology in recent critical works

Malcolm Bradbury and Judith Cooke (eds.), *New Writing*, Minerva, 1992
In an interview with Lorna Sage, Carter talks about carnival

Joseph Bristow and Trev Lynn Broughton (eds.), *The Infernal Desires of Angela Carter: Fiction, Femininity, Feminism*, Longman, 1997
A collection of essays focusing on Carter's use of **magic realism** and exploration of feminist and gender issues

David K. Danow, *The Spirit of Carnival: Magic Realism and the Grotesque*, University of Kentucky Press, 1995 (updated 2004)
Explores carnival and magical realism through medieval folk culture and modern texts

Aidan Day, *Angela Carter: The Rational Glass*, Manchester University Press, 1998
Chronological examination of Carter's fiction with clear accounts of influences and theoretical interpretations

Michael Dobson and Stanley Wells (eds.), *The Oxford Companion to Shakespeare*, Oxford University Press, 2001
Gives a detailed synopsis of *A Midsummer Night's Dream*, together with its stage, film and television history

Margaret Drabble (ed.), *The Oxford Companion to English Literature*, sixth edition, 2000

Alison Easton (ed.), *Angela Carter: Contemporary Critical Essays*, New Casebooks Series, Palgrave Macmillan, 2000
Contains a number of essays on specific texts with one chapter on *Wise Children*, Kate Webb's 'Seriously Funny: *Wise Children*', which also appears in *Flesh and the Mirror*, edited by Lorna Sage

Michel Foucault, *Archaeology of Knowledge*, Pantheon, 1972

Betty Friedan, *The Feminine Mystique*, Penguin, 1992

Sarah Gamble, *Angela Carter: Writing from the Front Line*, Edinburgh University Press, 1997

FURTHER READING

CRITICISM AND BACKGROUND READING continued

Sarah Gamble, *Angela Carter: A Literary Life*, Macmillan, 2005

Sarah Gamble (ed.), *The Fiction of Angela Carter: A Reader's Guide to Essential Criticism*, Palgrave Macmillan, 2001
As its title suggests, a comprehensive survey of critical approaches to Carter's fiction

Sarah Gamble (ed.), *The Routledge Companion to Feminism and Postfeminism*, Routledge, 2001 (updated 2006)

Linda Gordon, 'What's New in Women's History?', in *Feminist Studies/Critical Studies*, edited by Teresa de Laurentis, Indiana University Press, 1994
A much quoted essay on the status of women in modern society

Germaine Greer, *The Female Eunuch*, Flamingo, 1999 (first published 1970)

Germaine Greer, *The Whole Woman*, Doubleday, 1999

John Haffenden, *Novelists in Interview*, Methuen, 1985
Contains first-hand material from Angela Carter

Michael Hardin, 'The Other Other: Self-Definition Outside Patriarchal Institutions in Angela Carter's *Wise Children*', in *Review of Contemporary Fiction*, Volume 14, 1994
Explores the definition of the female outside of male structures in *Wise Children*, and examines the common individuality of Dora and Nora and their public and private identities

D. L. Kirkpatrick with James D. Vinson (eds.), *Contemporary Novelists*, Palgrave Macmillan, 1986

Michael McKeon (ed.), *Theory of the Novel: A Historical Approach*, Johns Hopkins University Press, 2000

Richard Maltby (ed.), *Dreams for Sale: Popular Culture in the Twentieth Century*, Harrap, 1989

Kate Millett, *Sexual Politics*, Doubleday, 1970
A key text on the development of modern feminism

Brian Moon, *Literary Terms: A Practical Glossary*, Chalkface Press, 1992
A glossary with helpful activities for students to broaden understanding of technical terms in critical analysis

Edward Muir, *Ritual in Early Modern Europe*, Cambridge University Press, 1997
Background reading for carnival in Europe

Susan Onega (ed.), *In Telling Histories: Narrativizing History, Historicizing Literature*, Rodopi, 1995
This collection of essays includes one by Celestine Deleyto entitled 'We are no Angels: Woman Versus History in Angela Carter's *Wise Children*'

Susan Osborne, *Feminism*, Pocket Essentials, 2001

Linden Peach, *Angela Carter*, Palgrave Macmillan, 1997
Looks at the magical and the realist elements in Carter's works to reveal her cultural and social explorations

Jeffrey Roessner, 'Writing a History of Difference: Jeanette Winterson's *Sexing the Cherry* and Angela Carter's *Wise Children*', in *College Literature*, Winter 2002
Examines the similarities of subject and theme but distinct feminine perspectives in these two novels

Lorna Sage, *Contemporary Writers: Angela Carter*, Book Trust for the British Council, 1980
Deals primarily with the formative ideas in Carter's earlier works

Lorna Sage, *Women in the House of Fiction: Post-War Women Novelists*, Palgrave Macmillan, 1992
Deals with Angela Carter in context of modern women novelists

Lorna Sage, *Angela Carter*, Northcote House Publishers, 1994
Contains an expanded version of Sage's article 'Death of the Author' (*Granta: Biography* 41, Autumn 1992)

Lorna Sage, *Moments of Truth: Twelve Twentieth-Century Writers*, HarperCollins, 2000
Carter is included in a study of modernism and women writers

Lorna Sage (ed.), *Flesh and the Mirror: Essays on the Art of Angela Carter*, Virago Press, 1994
A collection of essays on Angela Carter's work by several contributors

Simon Schama, *A History of Britain: The Fate of Empire*, Volume 3, BBC Worldwide, 2002

John Sears, *Angela Carter's Monstrous Women*, Sheffield Hallam University Press, 1992
Refers to other novels by Carter. Broader perspectives on feminism in Carter's earlier works

Tom Sobshack, 'Bakhtin's "carnivalesque" in 1950s British Comedy', in *Journal of Popular Film and Television*, Winter 1996

Michelene Wandor (ed.), *On Gender and Writing*, Pandora, 1983
Carter's 'Notes from the Front Line' can be found in this work

Kate Webb, 'Seriously Funny: *Wise Children*', in *Flesh and the Mirror: Essays on the Art of Angela Carter*, edited by Lorna Sage, Virago Press, 1994
A detailed essay covering the main themes and critical approaches in reading *Wise Children*

Jerry White, *London in the Twentieth Century: A City and Its People*, Viking, 2001

Gina Wisker, *Angela Carter: A Beginner's Guide*, Hodder and Stoughton, 2003
A brief overview of the variety of Angela Carter's work, narrative styles and themes with a section on *Wise Children*

Naomi Wolf, *The Beauty Myth*, Vintage, 1991

David Young and Keith Holloman (eds.), *Magic Realist Fiction: An Anthology*, Longman, 1984
Selected extracts and stories for wider reading across a range of authors

Lois Parkinson Zamora and Wendy B. Faris (eds.), *Magical Realism: Theory, History, Community*, Duke University Press, 1985
See Susan J. Napier's essay 'The Magic of Identity: Magical Realism in Modern Japanese Fiction'

allusion a reference to another work of literature, art form or any other topic, intended to add further meaning to a text

anticlimax the anticipated climax is missed and there is a sense of let-down which creates various effects, usually involving pathos or comedy

bathos an effect of anticlimax created by an unintentional lapse in mood from the sublime to the trivial or the ridiculous. Alexander Pope first used the word in this sense in his satire *Peri Bathous, or the art of sinking in poetry*

burlesque a form of theatre or music hall comedy and a form of literature which satirise a particular subject by creating a deliberate mismatch between the manner and the subject

carnivalesque a term which applies to the historical phenomenon of carnival but also to the inclusion of its elements in literary genres, particularly the novel

commedia dell'arte a type of comic drama evolved in sixteenth-century Italy using standard, recognisable plots

deconstruction a theory of literary criticism which suggests that a text has no absolute meaning and depends on interpretation. A text, therefore, is capable of several possible meanings. It is a central term in **post-structuralist** criticism

dialogism a term invented by the Russian critic Mikhail Bakhtin to identify the several voices within a literary text

farce a form of drama, though it can apply to any literary form, in which the comic is taken to extreme lengths of absurdity

Gothic in literature it is a form of Romanticism which deals with passion, horror, supernatural or mystery. It employs medieval settings or atmosphere, was popular in the late eighteenth and early nineteenth centuries and is enjoying a revival which began in the late twentieth century

intertextuality this term suggests that texts do not exist alone but have relationships with other texts. Comparison between texts, therefore, can enhance or expand meanings

irony saying or writing one thing but implying another; a situation where words are given meanings other than the literal or intended one. Irony, therefore, can be intended or unconscious

leitmotif (also **motif**) some aspect of literature which occurs frequently, with the intention of drawing attention to a particular theme or topic

magic realism fiction or other art forms such as painting or cinema which combine realism with fantastic elements. It reminds the reader or observer that all art is created/invented

melodrama a reinforcement of the emotional aspects of an art form. Originally stemming from the theatre, it can be applied to fiction and cinema and more recently to television. Used consciously it has a comic intention and effect, unconsciously a serious intention but a comic effect

memoirs an account of particular aspects or features of a writer's experiences

Menippean satire sometimes termed Varronian satire, this form is generally chaotic in form, where it is difficult to be specific about the targets of ridicule. (Menippus of Gadara was a Greek satirist and philosopher in the third century BC.) *Gargantua and Pantagruel* by Rabelais is often cited as an example, and the term has been used in critiques of Carter's works

motif see **leitmotif**

narrative a narrative is a story, tale or recital of facts, and refers to the **voice** or point of view or standpoint from which a story is related. First person ('I') uses a persona and usually requires the reader to judge carefully what is said. Second person ('you') suggests that the reader is a part of the action of the story. In a third-person narrative ('he', 'she', 'they') the narrator may be intrusive (continually commenting upon the story), impersonal, or omniscient. An omniscient narrator can control characters and situations, and be omnipresent and therefore godlike. At times a narrator will allow a narrative shift whereby another voice enters the narrative

parody deliberate imitation of another style or work of art usually for comic effect

pastiche a form of imitation which uses pieces of the work of another writer either for comic effect or for acknowledgement of quality

phallocentric literature a term from feminist criticism to define literature which implies or asserts male domination

polyphonic novel a term which devolves from **dialogism** and which indicates several **voices** within a novel

postmodernism a term which embraces other forms of criticism, notably feminism, Marxism and psychoanalytic criticism. As a literary movement, it follows from the threats to mankind of the mid twentieth century and reflects the doubts and fears of the period

post-structuralism a theory that suggests that the meaning of words is not absolute but varies with the context in which they are used

voice the persona(e) created by a writer to tell the story. Authorial voice may sometimes emerge in a text using persona(e)

AUTHOR OF THESE NOTES

Michael Duffy is a former English teacher with thirty-eight years' experience, teaching in both Canada and the UK. He has a degree from the University of Manchester and was Head of English at St Mary's College, Blackpool, for twenty-five years. He is a published author and a senior examiner.

NOTES

NOTES

Maya Angelou
I Know Why the Caged Bird Sings

Jane Austen
Pride and Prejudice

Alan Ayckbourn
Absent Friends

Elizabeth Barrett Browning
Selected Poems

Robert Bolt
A Man for All Seasons

Harold Brighouse
Hobson's Choice

Charlotte Brontë
Jane Eyre

Emily Brontë
Wuthering Heights

Brian Clark
Whose Life is it Anyway?

Robert Cormier
Heroes

Shelagh Delaney
A Taste of Honey

Charles Dickens
David Copperfield
Great Expectations
Hard Times
Oliver Twist
Selected Stories

Roddy Doyle
Paddy Clarke Ha Ha Ha

George Eliot
Silas Marner
The Mill on the Floss

Anne Frank
The Diary of a Young Girl

William Golding
Lord of the Flies

Oliver Goldsmith
She Stoops to Conquer

Willis Hall
The Long and the Short and the Tall

Thomas Hardy
Far from the Madding Crowd
The Mayor of Casterbridge
Tess of the d'Urbervilles
The Withered Arm and other Wessex Tales

L. P. Hartley
The Go-Between

Seamus Heaney
Selected Poems

Susan Hill
I'm the King of the Castle

Barry Hines
A Kestrel for a Knave

Louise Lawrence
Children of the Dust

Harper Lee
To Kill a Mockingbird

Laurie Lee
Cider with Rosie

Arthur Miller
The Crucible
A View from the Bridge

Robert O'Brien
Z for Zachariah

Frank O'Connor
My Oedipus Complex and Other Stories

George Orwell
Animal Farm

J. B. Priestley
An Inspector Calls
When We Are Married

Willy Russell
Educating Rita
Our Day Out

J. D. Salinger
The Catcher in the Rye

William Shakespeare
Henry IV Part I
Henry V
Julius Caesar
Macbeth
The Merchant of Venice
A Midsummer Night's Dream
Much Ado About Nothing
Romeo and Juliet
The Tempest
Twelfth Night

George Bernard Shaw
Pygmalion

Mary Shelley
Frankenstein

R. C. Sherriff
Journey's End

Rukshana Smith
Salt on the snow

John Steinbeck
Of Mice and Men

Robert Louis Stevenson
Dr Jekyll and Mr Hyde

Jonathan Swift
Gulliver's Travels

Robert Swindells
Daz 4 Zoe

Mildred D. Taylor
Roll of Thunder, Hear My Cry

Mark Twain
Huckleberry Finn

James Watson
Talking in Whispers

Edith Wharton
Ethan Frome

William Wordsworth
Selected Poems

A Choice of Poets

Mystery Stories of the Nineteenth Century including The Signalman

Nineteenth Century Short Stories

Poetry of the First World War

Six Women Poets

For the AQA Anthology:

Duffy and Armitage & Pre-1914 Poetry

Heaney and Clarke & Pre-1914 Poetry

Poems from Different Cultures

Margaret Atwood
Cat's Eye
The Handmaid's Tale

Jane Austen
Emma
Mansfield Park
Persuasion
Pride and Prejudice
Sense and Sensibility

William Blake
*Songs of Innocence and of
Experience*

Charlotte Brontë
Jane Eyre
Villette

Emily Brontë
Wuthering Heights

Angela Carter
Nights at the Circus
Wise Children

Geoffrey Chaucer
The Franklin's Prologue and Tale
The Miller's Prologue and Tale
*The Prologue to the Canterbury
Tales*
*The Wife of Bath's Prologue and
Tale*

Samuel Coleridge
Selected Poems

Joseph Conrad
Heart of Darkness

Daniel Defoe
Moll Flanders

Charles Dickens
Bleak House
Great Expectations
Hard Times

Emily Dickinson
Selected Poems

John Donne
Selected Poems

Carol Ann Duffy
Selected Poems

George Eliot
Middlemarch
The Mill on the Floss

T. S. Eliot
Selected Poems
The Waste Land

F. Scott Fitzgerald
The Great Gatsby

E. M. Forster
A Passage to India

Charles Frazier
Cold Mountain

Brian Friel
Translations
Making History

William Golding
The Spire

Thomas Hardy
Jude the Obscure
The Mayor of Casterbridge
The Return of the Native
Selected Poems
Tess of the d'Urbervilles

Seamus Heaney
*Selected Poems from 'Opened
Ground'*

Nathaniel Hawthorne
The Scarlet Letter

Homer
The Iliad
The Odyssey

Aldous Huxley
Brave New World

Kazuo Ishiguro
The Remains of the Day

Ben Jonson
The Alchemist

James Joyce
Dubliners

John Keats
Selected Poems

Christopher Marlowe
Doctor Faustus
Edward II

Ian McEwan
Atonement

Arthur Miller
Death of a Salesman

John Milton
Paradise Lost Books I & II

Toni Morrison
Beloved

George Orwell
Nineteen Eighty-Four

Sylvia Plath
Selected Poems

Alexander Pope
*Rape of the Lock & Selected
Poems*

William Shakespeare
Antony and Cleopatra
As You Like It
Hamlet
Henry IV Part I
King Lear
Macbeth
Measure for Measure
The Merchant of Venice
A Midsummer Night's Dream
Much Ado About Nothing
Othello
Richard II
Richard III
Romeo and Juliet
The Taming of the Shrew
The Tempest
Twelfth Night
The Winter's Tale

George Bernard Shaw
Saint Joan

Mary Shelley
Frankenstein

Bram Stoker
Dracula

Jonathan Swift
*Gulliver's Travels and A Modest
Proposal*

Alfred Tennyson
Selected Poems

Alice Walker
The Color Purple

Oscar Wilde
*The Importance of Being
Earnest*

Tennessee Williams
A Streetcar Named Desire

Jeanette Winterson
Oranges Are Not the Only Fruit

John Webster
The Duchess of Malfi

Virginia Woolf
To the Lighthouse

W. B. Yeats
Selected Poems

Metaphysical Poets